NATURAL GOODNESS

Natural Goodness

PHILIPPA FOOT

CLARENDON PRESS · OXFORD

OXFORD
UNIVERSITY PRESS

Great Clarendon Street, Oxford OX2 6DP

Oxford University Press is a department of the University of Oxford.
It furthers the University's objective of excellence in research, scholarship,
and education by publishing worldwide in

Oxford New York

Auckland Cape Town Dar es Salaam Hong Kong Karachi
Kuala Lumpur Madrid Melbourne Mexico City Nairobi
New Delhi Shanghai Taipei Toronto
With offices in
Argentina Austria Brazil Chile Czech Republic France Greece
Guatemala Hungary Italy Japan South Korea Poland Portugal
Singapore Switzerland Thailand Turkey Ukraine Vietnam

Oxford is a registered trade mark of Oxford University Press
in the UK and in certain other countries

Published in the United States
by Oxford University Press Inc., New York

ISBN 978-0-19-926547-3

Printed in the United Kingdom by
Lightning Source UK Ltd., Milton Keynes

To
Warren Quinn
In Memoriam

Man is indeed an object miraculous vain, various and wavering. It is difficult to found a judgement on him which is steady and uniform.

Montaigne, *Essays*, Book I, 1

You can attach the whole of moral philosophy to a commonplace private life just as well as to one of richer stuff. Every man bears the whole Form of the human condition.

Montaigne, *Essays*, Book III, 2

PREFACE

I have been writing this book for many years, and have benefited greatly from discussions with colleagues, especially at Oxford and UCLA, but also at many other universities. If I have here repeated other people's arguments without acknowledgement I only hope they will blame a defective memory rather than professional thievishness.

It will be obvious that I owe most to the work of Elizabeth Anscombe, and to early discussions with her. But I must also give special thanks to Christopher Coope, Peter Conradi, and Michael Thompson who read the whole of a first draft of the book and sent me wonderful comments. Anselm Müller has also read some chapters for me and helped me a great deal, and I have had many good discussions with John Campbell, Rosalind Hursthouse, and Gavin Lawrence.

Finally, I am extraordinarily grateful to Peter Momtchiloff at the Oxford University Press for his unfailing encouragement and patience, and to Angela Blackburn, whose editing has saved me from many blunders.

Oxford, May 2000 PRF

CONTENTS

Introduction

What is this book about? It is a book of *moral* philosophy, which means that we must discuss right and wrong and virtue and vice, the traditional subjects of moral judgement. But being a book of *philosophy*, it has to do only with a peculiar type of question about these subjects that is perhaps best identified either by example or by the special kind of malaise that we feel when examples of it appear.[1] Wittgenstein wrote of thinking that one cannot see one's way around, saying 'We feel as if we had to repair a torn spider's web with our fingers.'[2] And while on the topic of philosophy in general and Wittgenstein's philosophy in particular, I should like to take this chance to pass on a piece of advice that I have kept in mind throughout the writing of this book, remembering it as his on one of the two occasions when he took part in a public discussion in Oxford. Wittgenstein interrupted a speaker who had realized that he was about to say something that, although it seemed compelling, was clearly ridiculous, and was trying (as we all do in such circumstances) to say something sensible instead. 'No,' said Wittgenstein. 'Say what you *want* to say. Be *crude* and then we shall get on.' The suggestion that in doing philosophy one should not try to banish or tidy up a ludicrously crude but troubling thought, but rather give it its day, its week, its month, in court, seems to me very helpful. It chimes of course with Wittgenstein's idea that in philosophy it is very difficult to work as slowly as one should.

---

[1] The first such problem—later identified as philosophical—that I remember worrying about was when a grown-up used the words 'If I were you', and I wondered how we should notice the difference if she *were* me!

[2] Wittgenstein, *Philosophical Investigations*, section 106.

No one doubts, I think, that there are peculiarly philosophical difficulties in understanding ordinary moral judgements, because questions such as 'Why should I do what is right and good?' arise naturally and yet are so hard to understand. One feels that there must be something wrong with this question, but cannot say what it is that is wrong. Later I shall discuss this very problem, but the argument must start a long way back, and the starting point is crucial. We might be inclined to start, as for instance G. E. Moore did one hundred years ago in his vastly influential *Principia Ethica,* by fixing our eyes on the peculiarity of *goodness* when predicated as a property in a sentence such as 'Pleasure is good';[3] but I believe that to take such a starting point is to skew the enquiry from the outset. If in everyday life someone said to us 'Pleasure is good', we should ask, 'How do you mean?'—indicating that as it stands the proposition seems void for uncertainty, as a lawyer might say.

Moore regularly speaks of the judgement that a certain thing—pleasure, for instance, or friendship—'is good', as if 'X is good' could be taken as the standard form of predication for it, as for 'X is red'. It seems to me, however, extremely important that this should be challenged before we start on the usual discussions of the way in which Moore himself thought that goodness was a special kind of property (a 'non-naturalistic' property) and the theories that developed out of this thought. For the acceptance of this rarely appropriate form of words makes it hard to see the real logical grammar of evaluations, in which, in most contexts, 'good' requires to be complemented by a noun that plays an essential role in determining whether we are able to speak of goodness rather than badness, or indeed of goodness or badness at all. Peter Geach made this point in a sadly neglected article entitled 'Good and Evil', where he puts 'good' in the class of attributive adjectives, to which, for example, 'large' and 'small' belong, contrasting such adjectives with 'predicative' adjectives such as 'red'.[4] Such a colour word operates in in-

---

[3] Moore, *Principia Ethica,* e.g. chapter I, sections 3 and 9.

[4] I have sometimes secured instant recognition of this point by holding up a small bit of torn paper in front of an audience and asking them to say whether or not *it is good.* An offer to pass it round so that they can see it better gets a laugh that recognizes a logical—grammatical—absurdity.

dependence of any noun to which it is attached, but whether a particular F is a good F depends radically on what we substitute for 'F'. As 'large' must change to 'small' when we find that what we thought was a mouse was a rat, so 'bad' may change to 'good' when we consider a certain book of philosophy first as a book of philosophy and then as a soporific. Seen in the light of Geach's distinction, thoughts about good actions, which are fundamental to moral philosophy, appear with thoughts about good sight, good food, good soil, or good houses.

Geach's insistence that 'good' and 'red' are logically different is very important and takes us some of the way in the task of bringing back words 'from their metaphysical to their everyday use', as Wittgenstein said was characteristic of his own late philosophy.[5] But as Geach would, I am sure, agree, there are further distinctions of logical grammar to be made before we shall have identified the category to which moral evaluation belongs. What I mean here by a logical category of evaluation can be illustrated by the contrast between evaluating, say, a house from a utilitarian point of view, when questions such as 'for whom?' will have to be answered before an evaluation can be made or, by contrast, evaluating a house aesthetically, when this question would be out of place. These are two different logical categories in which evaluations can be made, and the aim of this book is to find that other one to which the moral evaluation of human actions belongs.

My constructive task is therefore to describe a particular type of evaluation and to argue that moral evaluation of human action is of this logical type. I am going to write about what may conveniently be called 'natural goodness and defect in living things', and this explains the title of my book; but the conjunction merely marks a term of art invented for the sake of convenience, and the sense of the expression will have to be given later on. In this brief introduction I shall go no further than to remark that by natural goodness I emphatically do not mean the goodness thought by many to belong, for instance, to some but not other sexual practices because some but not others are 'natural'. What I do mean is goodness of an indi-

[5] Wittgenstein, *Philosophical Investigations*, section 116.

vidual living thing (or of some characteristic or operation of it) as evaluated in a way that is not, I believe, sufficiently distinguished in moral philosophy, although it is easily recognized that a living thing can be evaluated in other logically different ways, as by its usefulness or dangerousness to us, or by its beauty or ugliness. My general thesis is that moral judgement of human actions and dispositions is one example of a genre of evaluation itself actually characterized by the fact that its objects are living things; though much more must be said later about that.

1

A Fresh Start?

For better or worse—and many will say worse—I have in this book the overt aim of setting out a view of moral judgement very different from that of most moral philosophers writing today. For I believe that evaluations of human will and action share a conceptual structure with evaluations of characteristics and operations of other living things, and can only be understood in these terms. I want to show moral evil as 'a kind of natural defect'. *Life* will be at the centre of my discussion, and the fact that a human action or disposition is good of its kind will be taken to be simply a fact about a given feature of a certain kind of living thing.

To make such a suggestion, as I interpret it, is to contemplate a naturalistic theory of ethics: to break really radically both with G. E. Moore's anti-naturalism and with the subjectivist theories such as emotivism and prescriptivism that have been seen as clarifications and developments of Moore's original thought. To get so much as a hearing for such a position, I must first describe, and give reasons for rejecting, the subjectivism that for the past sixty years or so has dominated moral philosophy in Britain, America, and other countries in which analytic philosophy is taught. This is the subjectivism—often called 'non-cognitivism'—that came to the fore with A. J. Ayer, C. L. Stevenson, and Richard Hare, informed the work of John Mackie and many others, and has lately appeared, refreshed, in Allan Gibbard's 'expressivist' account of normative language. Simon Blackburn, reviewing Gibbard's *Wise Choices, Apt Feelings*, has said that he hopes this book will now set the agenda for moral philosophy.[1] I myself, for all my admiration for Gibbard, hope that it

[1] See Blackburn, 'Wise Feelings, Apt Reading', 356.

will not do that. So I should say why I believe that these non-cognitivist theories—one and all—are based on a mistake.

To identify the common characteristic of the apparently some-what diverse moral philosophies that I have just grouped together, and also to do justice to them, it will be good to start by asking how the whole non-cognitivist business began. One finds its deepest roots in David Hume. But more immediately, Ayer and Stevenson's emotivism, like Hare's prescriptivism, came into being as a result of the 'linguistic turn', popularized by logical positivism but developing far beyond it. For with 'linguistic philosophy' came the idea of explaining the singularity of moral judgement in terms of a special use of language, called 'evaluation' but more akin to exclamation and command than to anything one would normally mean by that term. With this idea it seemed possible, at last, to say clearly what G. E. Moore had meant, or should have meant, when he insisted that goodness was a special kind of 'non-natural' property.[2] In the development of emotivism and prescriptivism the idea of a special ('non-natural') property was replaced by that of a special and essen-tially practical use of language. And this, it seemed, was a great dis-covery. The language of evaluation was 'emotive'. It expressed a speaker's feelings and attitudes, as well as inducing similar feelings and attitudes in others. Those who had these 'attitudes' 'favoured' the things they called 'good': the idea of an attitude being linked to a tendency to act. Such also was Ayer's doctrine; and a little later Hare tied 'evaluation' even more closely to individual action, in his theory of universalized imperatives by which a speaker exhorted others and, in the acceptance of a first-person imperative, commit-ted himself to choose what he called 'good'. So 'prescriptivism'—a distinctive version of the doctrine that I have in my sights—was added to the emotivism with which it had started out. In an explicit definition of the 'prescriptive' use of language, Hare wrote:

We say something prescriptive if and only if, for some act A, some situation S and some person P, if P were to assent (orally) to what we say, and not, in S, do A, he logically must be assenting insincerely.[3]

---

[2] Moore, *Principia Ethica*. See, especially, chapter II, section 26, and chapter IV, sec-tion 73.　　　　　　　　　　　　　　　　　　　　[3] Hare, *Moral Thinking*, 21.

I shall come back to this definition later on. First, I should say something more general about the theories I am attacking. It is characteristic of those I have mentioned and others inspired by them to suggest that the making of any sincere moral judgement requires the presence of individual feeling, attitude, or intention, and thus goes beyond 'description' or 'assertion of fact'. It was recognized, of course, that the language contains many terms like 'courage' or 'justice' designed for description *as well as* moral judgement, but it was said that their 'descriptive' content could not reach all the way to moral evaluation; the speaker's feelings or commitments to action would have to be added if evaluation were to be on the scene. Hence the apparently unquestionable distinction between 'descriptive' and 'evaluative' language, more or less taken for granted in much of contemporary ethics.

In early versions of these theories it was suggested that only a demand for consistency set any limits on the classes of actions to which words such as 'morally good' or 'morally bad' could be applied. So the extra feature supposedly involved in moral judgement could stand on its own, ready to form the core of alien moral systems confronting, or even directly contradicting, our own; if no linguistic device existed for expressing 'moral approval' or 'moral disapproval' in their purity, this was held to be merely an accident of language. Thus these early theories were radically subjectivist, allowing the possibility even of bizarre so-called 'moral judgements' about the wrongness of running around trees right-handed or looking at hedgehogs in the light of the moon, and so opening up limitless possibilities of irresolvable moral conflict. Nowadays it is commonly admitted, I believe, that there is some content restriction on what can intelligibly be said to be a system of morality. Moreover, Hare himself has suggested that a fairly tight form of utilitarianism can actually be obtained from universalized prescriptivism.[4] So it is not the old battle against a 'free-for-all' subjectivism that I want to fight. I find my target in the later, as in the earlier, versions of non-cognitivism. Even if the very tightest limitations on 'descriptive content' were accepted—even Bentham's suggestion that when used in

---

[4] Hare, *Freedom and Reason,* especially chapter 7.

conjunction with the greatest happiness principle, words such as 'ought' and 'right' have meaning, and otherwise not—'description' would still not, according to these theories, reach all the way to moral judgement.[5] Someone convinced of the utility—or whatever—of certain kinds of action would not—indeed could not—straightforwardly and with sincerity make the judgement about their moral goodness unless he found in himself the right feelings and attitudes, or was ready to take the step of committing himself to act in a particular way. For moral evaluation, something 'conative' had to be present as well as belief in matters of fact.

What all these theories tried to do, then, was to give the *conditions of use* of sentences such as 'It is morally objectionable to break promises' in terms of something that must be true about the speaker. He must have certain feelings or attitudes; he must commit himself to acting in a certain way; he must at least feel remorse if he does not so act. *Meaning was thus to be explained in terms of a speaker's attitude, intentions, or state of mind.* And this opened up a gap between moral judgements and assertions, with the idea that truth conditions give, and may exhaust, the meaning of the latter but not the former. Thus it seemed that *fact*, complementary to assertion, had been distinguished from *value*, complementary to the expression of feeling, attitude, or commitment to action. Propositions about matters of fact were assertable if their truth conditions were fulfilled, but moral judgements, through conditions of utterance, were essentially linked to an individual speaker's subjective state.

It is this kind of thing that seems to me all wrong, and to which I referred in the lecture 'Does Moral Subjectivism Rest on a Mistake?' on which this chapter is based. So what, then, is the mistake? It is the mistake of so construing what is 'special' about moral judgement that the grounds of a moral judgement do not reach all the way to it. Whatever 'grounds' may have been given, someone may be unready, indeed unable, to make the moral judgement, because he has not *got* the attitude or feeling, is not *in* the 'conative' state of mind, is not *ready to* take the decision to act: whatever it is that the

---

[5] See Bentham, *An Introduction to the Principles of Morals and Legislation*, chapter 1, paragraph 10.

theory says is required. It is this gap between ground and moral judgement that I am denying. In my view there are no such conditions on moral judgement and therefore no such gap.

It was not, however, a fit of collective madness that seized moral philosophers in the mid-twentieth century, and still grips them today. Their theories were devised to take account of something that really is a feature of moral judgement: the 'action-guiding' character of morality, which Hume had insisted on and taken as the foundation of his moral philosophy. Morality, Hume had said, is necessarily practical, serving to produce and prevent action, and I shall call this 'Hume's practicality requirement'.[6] Nor am I denying that his demand must be met. My contention is rather that the theories I am attacking tried to meet it in the wrong way. This, substantially, is what this chapter is about.

If I am to prove my thesis I must, of course, produce an alternative to the non-cognitivist way of showing that moral judgement is essentially 'action-guiding'. So what is my own account of the matter? It is, to state it briefly, that Hume's demand is met by the (most un-Humean) thought that acting morally is part of practical rationality.

Now I am quite aware that to make this suggestion will seem most foolhardy: a case of putting one's head, philosophically speaking, into the lion's mouth. For is it not difficult to establish even the coincidence of moral and rational action? What, after all, about those problem cases where justice or charity forbids the only way out of a tight corner, and the life of the agent may even be at stake? Isn't the demonstration of the rationality of just action a problem with which David Gauthier, for instance, has been wrestling for years, with great energy and skill?[7] And isn't this the fence at which I myself have repeatedly fallen, trying now this way, now that, of getting over—from 'Moral Beliefs' in 1958 to 'Morality as a System of Hypothetical Imperatives' in 1972? All of this is true, and if I am hopeful of greater success this time round it is because I think I now

---

[6] See Hume, *A Treatise of Human Nature*, Book III, part I, section 1, and *An Enquiry Concerning the Principles of Morals*, section 1.

[7] See Gauthier, *Morals by Agreement*.

see why I couldn't have managed it before. Roughly speaking, it was because I still held a more or less Humean theory of reasons for action, taking it for granted that reasons had to be based on an agent's desires. To be sure, in another article written in 1972 I had (rather inconsistently with my doubts about the rational status of morals) allowed considerations of self-interest an independent 'reason-giving' force.[8] But this didn't help with the rationality of disinterested justice, which rationality I was, rather scandalously, inclined to restrict to those whose desires were such as to allow them to be described as lovers of justice. I have therefore, rightly, been accused by my critics of reintroducing subjectivity at the level of rationality while insisting on objectivity in the criteria of moral right and wrong.

In common with others, I took it for granted at that time that a discussion of the rationality of moral action would start from some theory or other about what a reason for action must be: rather favouring a desire-fulfilment theory, with some special allowance for the force of considerations of self-interest. I now believe that both the self-interest theory of rationality and the theory of rationality as desire fulfilment are mistaken. Moreover, there seems to be a mistake of *strategy* involved in trying to fit the rationality of moral action into either theory: such an enterprise implying that we first come to a theory of rational action, and then try as best we can to slot in the rationality of acts of justice and charity.

That this was a mistake of strategy was suggested to me by my friend Warren Quinn, and while I do not think that he really developed the idea himself, the same thought is implicit in his attack on end-neutral, Humean, theories of rationality, in an important article, 'Putting Rationality in its Place', reprinted following his very sadly early death in the collection of his papers called *Morality and Action*. What, asked Quinn, would be *so important* about practical rationality if it were rational to seek to fulfil any, even a despicable, desire? In asking this he was questioning whether it is right to think that moral action has to be brought under a pre-established concept of practical rationality, and this seems to me to be very important

---

[8] Foot, 'Reasons for Action and Desire'.

indeed. My own view is, and perhaps his was, that there is no question here of 'fitting in' *in this direction*. I do not, therefore, want to canvas the rival claims of self-interest or maximum satisfaction of desires as accounts of practical rationality, and then try, as Gauthier and many others do, to explain the rationality of moral action in terms of the one that wins out. But nor do I think, on the other side, that the whole of practical rationality can be brought under the umbrella of 'morality', as we usually understand that term.

As I see it, the rationality of, say, telling the truth, keeping promises, or helping a neighbour is *on a par* with the rationality of self-preserving action, and of the careful and cognizant pursuit of other innocent ends; each being a part or aspect of practical rationality. The different considerations are on a par, moreover, in that a judgement about what is required by practical rationality must take account of their interaction: of the weight of the ones we call nonmoral as well as those we call moral. For it is not always rational to give help where it is needed, to keep a promise, or even, I believe, always to speak the truth. If it is to be said that 'moral considerations' are always 'overriding', it cannot be these particular considerations that we refer to, but must rather be the overall judgement about what, all things considered, should be done. Sorting out this particular point of precedence is, I think, a matter of keeping one's head and remembering that some expressions do and some do not imply overall judgement: imprudence, for instance, being by definition contrary to rationality, but self-sacrifice not. Leaving aside this complication, we may think of the different requirements of rationality in action as on a par. I shall argue later that there is a unity to these different grounds of practical rationality that may not be obvious right away. What I want to stress at this point is that in my account of the relation between goodness of choice and practical rationality it is the former that is primary. I want to say, baldly, that there is no criterion for practical rationality that is not *derived from* that of goodness of the will.

How, I shall be asked, can that be so, given that promises must often be kept, truth told, or succour given, even when that is contrary to self-interest or to heart's desire?

The demonstration may start, I believe, with some observations on the nature of a virtue. It is in the concept of a virtue that in so far as someone possesses it, his actions are good; which is to say that he acts well. Virtues bring it about that one who has them acts well, and we must enquire as to what this does and does not mean.

What, for instance, distinguishes a just person from one who is unjust? The fact that he keeps his contracts? That cannot be right, because circumstances may make it impossible for him to do so. Nor is it that he saves life rather than kills innocent people, for by blameless mishap he may kill rather than save. 'Of course,' someone will say at this point, 'it is the just person's intention, not what he actually brings about, that counts.' But why not say, then, that it is the distinguishing characteristic of the just that *for them certain considerations count as reasons for action, and as reasons of a given weight*? Will it not be the same with other virtues, as for instance for the virtues of charity, courage, and temperance? Those who possess these virtues possess them in so far as they recognize certain considerations (such as the fact of a promise, or of a neighbour's need) as powerful, and in many circumstances compelling, reasons for acting. They recognize the reasons, and act on them.

Thus the description 'just', as applied to a man or a woman, speaks of how it is with him or her in respect of the acceptance of a certain group of considerations as reasons for action. If justice is a virtue, this is what the virtue of justice rectifies, that is, makes good. It is no part of the goodness that is goodness of the will that someone should be physically strong, should move well, talk well, or see well. But he must act well, in a sense that is given primarily at least by his recognition of the force of particular considerations as reasons for acting: that and the influence that this has on what he does. The just person *aims* at keeping promises, paying what is owed, and defending those whose rights are being violated, so far as such actions are required by the virtue of justice. Likewise, he recognizes certain limitations on what he may do even for some virtue-given end; as he may not kill an innocent person even for the sake of stopping someone else from killing a greater number, though he may (to use one of Elizabeth Anscombe's many memorable examples) destroy someone's property to stop the spread of a fire. And again he acts accordingly. Similarly, if charity is a virtue, this is because it makes its possessor's action good in the area of aims such as the relief of poverty. Here again, recognizing particular considerations as reasons for action, he acts on these reasons as he should.[9]

Now in describing virtues in terms of (a) the recognition of particular considerations as reasons for acting, and (b) the relevant action, I have only been expressing familiar and time-honoured ideas of moral goodness. But how can it be denied that I have at the same time been talking about practical rationality? The discussion has been about human goodness in respect of reason-recognition and reason-following, and if this is not practical rationality I should like to know what is. The reply from those who hold a preconceived theory of practical rationality will be, no doubt, that rationality is the following of perceived self-interest; alternatively, that it is the pursuit, careful and cognizant, of the maximum satisfaction of present desires; each respondent suggesting that one of these rival theories gives *the* concept of practical rationality. At the very least, they may argue, such theories give a valid alternative idea of practical rationality, to set beside the one that emerged from our discussion of justice and charity as virtues having to do with the following of reasons. But I suggested earlier that this was a mistake: that we should not think in terms of rival theories, but of the different parts of practical rationality, no one of which should be mistaken for the whole. An action can be contrary to practical rationality in that it is dishonest or disrespectful of others' rights, *or* that it is foolishly imprudent; *or*, again, that the agent is, for example, careless, timid, or half-hearted in going for what he wants.

Given that there are at least so many different cases, which it may or may not be useful to categorize, it is not surprising that the blanket term 'practical irrationality', and cognates such as 'contrary to practical reason', may go along with different subsidiary descriptions. I do not want to argue about bits of linguistic usage: about where, for instance, the particular term 'irrational', or again 'unreasonable', is or isn't at home. It is obvious that some terms such as 'silly' or 'foolish', and even 'irrational' in its common use, do not

---

[9] The fact that possession of a virtue carries implications that go beyond actions or even intentions is given explicit recognition later in this book. See Chapter 4.

correctly describe the actions of, for instance, the Great Train Robbers; even though in being dishonest, and criminally careless of the life of the train driver, what they did was contrary to justice and so, in the view I am expounding, to practical rationality. It makes for nothing but confusion to centre an argument about practical reason around one particular expression cut off from its genuine application, as Allan Gibbard did in supposing moral judgement to be expressible in terms of what does or does not 'make sense':[10] as if *that* were the way to say what was wrong with the train robbers' actions, or with the notoriously extortionist English landlord Rachmann's dealings with his tenants!

There is no doubt but that there are different kinds of cases of contrary-to-reason-ness, and not surprisingly it is possible to contravene rationality in more than one way at the same time. I once read of a burglar who was caught because he sat down to watch television in the house he was burgling, thus adding the contrary-to-reason-ness of imprudence to that of dishonesty. Because his actions were faulty in that he did not hurry away with the swag, we can say, if we like, that he *should* have done so. It does not follow, however, that he would have acted well if he had avoided imprudence, because no one can act with full practical rationality in the pursuit of a bad end.[11]

It is, I think, possible to see, even if not as yet very clearly, the common thread linking these different parts of practical rationality. The root notion is that of the goodness of human beings in respect of their actions; which means, to repeat, goodness of the will rather than of such things as sight, dexterity, or memory. Kant was perfectly right in saying that moral goodness was goodness of the will; the idea of practical rationality is throughout a concept of this kind. He seems to have gone wrong, however, in thinking that an abstract idea of practical reason applicable to rational beings as such could take us all the way to anything like our own moral code. For the evaluation of human action depends also on essential features of specifically human life.

[10] See Gibbard, *Wise Choices, Apt Feelings*, for instance, pp. 7, 37, 38.
[11] See Chapter 4 of the present book.

Elizabeth Anscombe brings out this dependence of morality on the life of our species in a passage in her article 'On Promising and its Justice'. There she points out facts about human life that make it necessary for human beings to be able to bind each other to action through institutions like promising, such as that there are so few other ways in which one person can reliably get another to do what he wants. And what hangs on this may, we might add, be something very important, such as that one's children should be cared for after one's death. I shall consider Anscombe's discussion of promising at more length in Chapter 3.

Anscombe writes, '[G]etting one another to do things without the application of physical force is a necessity for human life, and that far beyond what could be secured by . . . other means.'[12] Anscombe is pointing here to what she has elsewhere called an 'Aristotelian necessity': that which is necessary because and in so far as good hangs on it.[13] We invoke the same idea when we say that it is necessary for plants to have water, for birds to build nests, for wolves to hunt in packs, and for lionesses to teach their cubs to kill. These 'Aristotelian necessities' depend on what the particular species of plants and animals need, on their natural habitat, and the ways of making out that are in their repertoire. These things together determine what it is for members of a particular species to be as they should be, and to do that which they should do.[14] And for all the enormous differences between the life of humans and that of plants or animals, we can see that human defects and excellences are similarly related to what human beings are and what they do. We do not need to be able to dive like gannets, nor to see in the dark like owls; but our memory and concentration must be such as to allow us to learn language, and our sight such that we can recognize faces at a glance; while, like lionesses, human parents are defective if they do not teach their young the skills that they need to survive.

[12] Anscombe, 'On Promising and its Justice', *Collected Philosophical Papers*, iii. 18.

[13] See ibid. 15, 18–19; 'Rules, Rights and Promises', *Collected Philosophical Papers*, iii. 100–1; 'On the Source of the Authority of the State', *Collected Philosophical Papers*, iii. 139.

[14] I have written here of species, but it might be better to use the words 'life form' as Michael Thompson does. (Here I am particularly indebted to his work.)

Moreover, in that we are social animals, we depend on each other as do wolves that hunt in packs, with cooperation such as our own depending on special factors such as conventional arrangements. Like the animals, we do things that will benefit others rather than ourselves: there is no good case for assessing the goodness of human action by reference only to good that each person brings to himself. Is it, one wonders, some lingering shadow of the thoroughly discredited doctrine of psychological egoism—of the belief that all *human* action is directed to the good of the agent himself—that inclines us to an egoistic concept of practical rationality? I do not know what else should make us think that the evaluation of reason-following behaviour must be altogether different in its conceptual structure from the evaluation of the behaviour of an animal. And it will surely not be denied that there is something wrong with a free-riding wolf that feeds but does not take part in the hunt, as with a member of the species of dancing bees who finds a source of nectar but whose behaviour does not let other bees know of its location. These free-riding individuals of a species whose members work together are just as *defective* as those who have defective hearing, sight, or powers of locomotion.

I am therefore, quite seriously, likening the basis of moral evaluation to that of the evaluation of behaviour in animals. I should stress, however, that it is important not to underestimate the degree to which human communication and reasoning change the scene. The goods that hang on human cooperation, and hang too on such things as respect for truth, art, and scholarship, are much more diverse and much harder to delineate than are animal *goods*. Animals are different also from us in that to do what they should do—what is needed and is within their capacity—they do not have to understand what is going on; whereas a human being can and should understand that, and why, there is reason for, say, keeping a promise or behaving fairly. This last may seem a tall order, but this human understanding is not anything hard to come by. We all know enough to say. 'How could we get on without justice?', 'Where would we be if no one helped anyone else?', or 'How could we manage if there were no way of making decisions for us all?'

Anyone who thinks about it can see that for human beings the teaching and following of morality is something necessary. We can't get on without it. And this is the nub of the proper answer to the challenge that I made in 'Morality as a System of Hypothetical Imperatives', where I asked why it should be thought rational to follow morality, but not to obey duelling rules or silly rules of etiquette. In that article I myself made a rotten job of answering my own question because, still under the influence of Humean ideas of practical rationality, I thought irrelevant what is now turning out to be most relevant.[15]

Later on, Warren Quinn helped me by pointing out that after this change I could at least claim to have found the basis for a unified theory of rationality. For if the virtues nowadays thought of especially worthy to be called moral virtues, and often contrasted with prudence, are 'Aristotelian necessities' for human beings, so too is a reasonable modicum of self-interest, if only because, once grown, we can look out for ourselves much better than anyone else can do it for us.[16] Good hangs, too, on the careful and cognizant pursuit of many more particular ends, and in general in satisfying appetites and following desires.

It is time now for me to return to the main line of my argument against non-cognitivism. It is because I see practical rationality as determined in this way that I claim to be able to interpret the 'action-guidingness' of moral judgement in terms of the practical rationality of moral action. And please notice that I have not re-introduced, via the concept of practical rationality itself, a subjective (agent-centred) condition on moral judgement. For I have not subscribed to a desire-based, Humean, theory of practical rationality: nor have I any reason to go along with Gibbard's 'expressivist' account of what it is we are doing when we say that a certain action is rational. Nothing of that kind has had any part in what I have said.

[15] It was, I remember, a remark of Rosalind Hursthouse's in a discussion that put me right about this. See also Hursthouse, *On Virtue Ethics*, especially chapters 9 and 10.

[16] In theory, this could, of course, be different for some other kinds of rational beings. Perhaps they would find it impossible to think calmly about *their own* future, and would have invented a kind of 'buddy system' by which each person had someone else to look out for him. We should find this extremely inconvenient except in bringing up children when they are small.

If I am right, therefore, about judgements of practical rationality and their ground, and right in seeing the kind of thing that Elizabeth Anscombe said about promising as simply one particular application of general (*species-based*) criteria of evaluation, I can claim to see how, in principle, a non-subjectivist—indeed cognitivist—reply might be given to Hume's demand that morality be shown to be 'necessarily practical'. Considerations about such things as promising, neighbourliness, and help for those in trouble have, I maintain, the same kind of connection with reasons for action as do considerations of self-interest or of means to our ends: the connection going in each case through the concept of practical rationality and the facts of human life. So I think that we can see as hopeful the project of producing a cognitivist alternative to theories such as emotivism, prescriptivism, and expressivism: an alternative that takes care of just what they were trying to take care of, in the way of a necessary connection between moral judgement and action.

I am sure that it will be objected at this point that even if, along these lines, a certain conceptual link has been shown to hold between moral language and action, via the fact that a moral judgement speaks of what there is reason to do, this will not have put the connection in the right place. For, it will be said, a relation has not been shown that holds between moral judgement and the action of *each and every individual*. This, however, I would dispute. On a 'practical rationality' account, a moral judgement says something about the action of any individual to whom it applies: namely, something about the reason that there is for *him* to do it or not do it, whether or not he recognizes that, and whether or not, if he does recognize it, he also acts on it as he should. Moreover, it can explain moral action in an individual who knows that he has reason to act morally; because acting on reasons is a basic mode of operation in human beings. This, too, is part of my account of the way in which morality is necessarily practical: it serves to produce and prevent action, *because the understanding of reasons can do that.*

We must be careful, however, not to tie moral judgement too closely to action. One who is the subject of a true moral judgement does not always do what it says he should do, since he may not recognize its truth, and may not act on it even if he does. In spite of recognizing the force of Hume's 'practicality requirement', we must allow for ignorance, for weakness of will, and also for the phenomenon of shamelessness. It should be seen as an advantage, not a disadvantage, if my 'rationality' account leaves room for this last. No doubt quite open shamelessness is fairly rare (even today), at least in the circles in which most philosophers live. But it is important to recognize that shamelessness can coexist with the use of moral language, and to see that this shamelessness is not the same as insincerity. I have read, for instance, of a member of a group of city louts out for a day in the country to hunt down some small inoffensive animal, who, though described as 'the conscience of the group', said 'I know I'm on earth 70 years and that I'm not going anywhere else. If I choose to spend my day out in the countryside doing whatever I feel like, then that's what I'll do.' And again of a certain Brooklyn machine politician who had the gall to say that while people think it hard to stand up for what is right, what is really hard is what he was doing, 'standing up day after day, week after week, for what is wrong'. Like Alec D'Urberville in Hardy's novel, this politician might have said 'I have lived bad, and I shall die bad', meaning what he said, but without the slightest intention to reform.

There are, it is true, some who try to hide their shamelessness by making an attack on morality. But more people than we like to admit are simply shameless. Are they then not 'endorsing the norm' of justice and charity, to use Gibbard's words for what he sees as expressing a state of mind in moral judgement? Well, I do not know what is meant by this somewhat contrived expression. I suppose that most criminals do not think much about the topic of morality, being in this rather like the British politician who, when confronted with a nasty fact about the arms trade, is reported to have said 'I do not much fill my mind with what one set of foreigners does to another.' I suppose one can evade either 'endorsing' or not 'endorsing' morality, or part of morality, by simply refusing to think about it; and I suppose that most of us do that at times. But D'Urberville seems not, on the night he seduced Tess, to have pushed morality out of sight, when he said 'I have lived bad, and I shall die bad', and it is important to contrast his mentality with the point of view of those whom we may call '(ideological) immoralists', such as

Thrasymachus, Callicles, Nietzsche, or André Gide. For they queried whether human goodness and badness are what they are supposed to be, whereas D'Urberville implicitly endorsed ordinary moral opinion, as did the Brooklyn machine politician, and perhaps also the 'city hunter' who seems to have thought that there was reason for him to let harmless animals live. By contrast with these shameless individuals, the immoralists are bringing arguments in favour of some different standard of human goodness.

I am not, of course, denying that there are many ambiguous cases; but the two poles of shamelessness and immoralism nevertheless exist. And it is not the shameless, but those who in their heart of hearts agree with, say, Thrasymachus or Nietzsche, who are *insincere* if they speak as we do about what is right and wrong.

It follows, therefore, from the line of argument of this chapter that Hare, who said that moral language was 'prescriptive'—and who so defined the prescriptive use of language that anyone who assents to a prescriptive proposition that in circumstances C an action A is morally wrong, but nevertheless does A in C, is as a matter of logic insincere—said something that is not true.[17] Moral judgements, while we may want to call them 'prescriptive' for some other reason, are not 'prescriptive' *in this sense*.[18] So no good reason has so far been given for thinking that there is any kind of 'logical gap' between a moral judgement and its grounds.

At this point, however, I must return to the subject of the 'practicality' of morality, to see how my account of it works out in face of a rather different version of non-cognitivism that is popular today. I pointed out earlier that non-cognitivism starts out from the obviously correct idea that moral judgement has a special connection with the actions which, as Hume said, it 'serves to produce and prevent'. Nor is this a contingent connection. It is in the concept of morality that the thought that something ought to be done has a relation to action lacked by such thoughts as that the earth is round,

---

[17] For Hare's reply, see his 'Off on the Wrong Foot'.

[18] In another sense they are of course prescriptive, as are orders, rules, laws, warnings, codes of dress, and so on. As Christopher Coope has pointed out to me, there is, in a way, a 'practicality requirement' for very many parts of our language.

strawberries sweet, or many lives lost in wars. In this chapter I have accepted this premise but interpreted it differently, suggesting that it is because moral action is a requirement of practical rationality that it has a special connection with the will. But it is just here that some of my non-cognitivist opponents will move in, scenting victory. For they will insist that the fact of an agent's having reason to do something (say to keep promises) is itself dependent on his feelings, passions, or desires. And so, they will argue, if a moral judgement about what I ought to do implies that I have reason so to act, the judgement would seem to imply not just 'cognitions' but also something 'conative': something having to do with an engagement of the will. A non-cognitivist, neo-Humean theory of reasons for action is thus being called in to support a neo-Humean account of moral judgement.

To many of its contemporary proponents, this account of reasons for action will probably seem particularly telling against an account of the practical aspect of morality such as the one I have given. For they too think of one who makes a moral judgement as necessarily having reason to act. A person's moral views suffice on occasion to explain his action: the moral judgement gave him a 'motivating reason' to do what he did. And this, my opponents believe, implies a fact about him: a fact about his attitudes, feelings, or desires.

In the form in which this argument is now often put forward it begins, therefore, from the premise that moral judgements are 'motivating reasons' for action; by which it is meant that people do things simply because they think that they ought to do so. And this is followed by a particular account of what it is for anyone to have such a motivating, action-explaining, reason as part of his 'psychological state'.

The seductive power of this account of reasons for action is considerable. It rests, no doubt, on what John McDowell has called the mechanical or hydraulic picture of the psychological determinants of action: a picture of desires as forces moving the will in certain directions, with action the result of a combination of belief and desire.[19] Such a picture is just as suspect as McDowell says it is; but

[19] See McDowell, 'Are Moral Requirements Hypothetical Imperatives?', 8–9.

what, we must ask, ever gave us such a picture? Where does its seductiveness lie?

To answer this question it will be useful to consider an article by Michael Smith in which what he calls 'the Humean theory of motivation' is defended. He writes:

[T]he distinctive feature of a motivating reason to φ is that in virtue of having such a reason an agent is in a state that is *potentially explanatory* of his φing. . . . [And] it would seem to be part of our concept of what it is for an agent's reasons to have the potential to explain his behaviour that his having these reasons is a fact about *him*; that is, that the goals that such reasons embody are *his* goals.[20]

We are likely to be seduced by this because it is natural to think in the following way. Take as an example that of someone who throws away his supply of cigarettes. He does so because he wants to give up smoking. And he wants to give up smoking because he wants a healthy old age. The series goes on—A for the sake of B—but it can't go on forever.[21] Must it not end with something that the agent 'just wants'; in other words, with some 'conative' element in his individual psychological state?

The question is meant to be rhetorical; but the answer to it is 'No'. For what, we must ask, gives the agent this goal? Does he find himself trembling at the thought of cancer at 50? Is he in a state of anxiety at the thought of how much he smokes? Perhaps. But nothing of this kind has to be part of the story, as Smith himself admits. So why do we say that what gets the whole thing going must be a desire or other 'conative' element in the subject's 'psychological state'? Suppose instead that it is the recognition that there is reason for him, as for anyone else, to look after his future so far as circumstances allow? Why should not this be where the series of questions 'Why?' comes to an end? Those already in thrall to the mechanical picture of the workings of the mind will deny it. Others may, however, consider the question *why should we not take the recognition of a reason for acting as bringing the series to a close?* Recognition of a reason

---

[20] Smith, 'The Humean Theory of Motivation', 38.
[21] Cp. Hume, *An Enquiry Concerning the Principles of Morals*, Appendix I.

gives the rational person a goal; and this recognition is, according to the argument of the present chapter, based on facts and concepts, not on some prior attitude, feeling, or goal. The only fact about the individual's state of mind that is required for the explanatory force of the proposition about the requirement of rationality is that he does not (for some bizarre reason) deny its truth. He only needs to know, like most adults, that it is silly to disregard one's own future without special reason to do so. No special explanation is needed of why men take reasonable care of their own future; an explanation is needed when they do not. Nor does human cooperation need a special explanation. Most people know that it is, for instance, unreasonable to take benefits and give nothing in return.

In denying the neo-Humean account of reasons for action in general it is, however, important to stress that there are some that do depend on what a particular person wants. If I want to see the Taj Mahal, I have reason to buy a ticket to India as someone who detests all things Eastern does not. The imperative is, as Kant would say, hypothetical: if I no longer want to see India, the reason may well disappear. Another obvious example is that of someone who, feeling hungry and having no food in the house, goes down the road to buy something to eat. If he were not hungry, he would not have this reason to go, and unless there were some other reason in the offing, the facts about the food shop and the empty larder could not explain why he went to the shop.

My conclusion is, therefore, that neither directly (through conditions on sincere moral utterances) nor indirectly (through the thought that moral judgement can explain action) does the acceptance of 'Hume's practicality requirement' give any support to noncognitivism in ethics. Nor has any reason been given for the existence of a logical gap between a moral judgement and its grounds. The premises of a moral argument give grounds for an assertion about what it is morally good—and therefore about what it is practically rational—to do. And *for anything that has been shown to the contrary*, these premises could even entail the conclusion, though I have certainly not argued that this is so. I have very little idea of how much 'play' there will in the end turn out to be in disagreements between moralities, and how many grey areas and irreconcilable opinions we shall want to recognize. One can keep an open mind about that.

What, then, is to be said about the relation between 'fact' and 'value'? The thesis of this chapter is that the grounding of a moral argument is ultimately in facts about human life—facts of the kind that Anscombe mentioned in talking about the good that hangs on the institution of promising, and of the kind that I spoke of in saying why it was a part of rationality for human beings to take special care each for his or her own future. In my view, therefore, a moral evaluation does not stand over against the statement of a matter of fact, but rather has to do with facts about a particular subject matter, as do evaluations of such things as sight and hearing in animals, and other aspects of their behaviour. Nobody would, I think, take it as other than a plain matter of fact that there is something wrong with the hearing of a gull that cannot distinguish the cry of its own chick, as with the sight of an owl that cannot see in the dark. Similarly, it is obvious that there are objective, factual evaluations of such things as human sight, hearing, memory, and concentration, based on the life form of our own species. Why, then, does it seem so monstrous a suggestion that the evaluation of the human will should be determined by facts about the nature of human beings and the life of our own species? Undoubtedly the resistance has something to do with the thought that the goodness of good action has a special relation to choice. But as I have tried to show, this special relation is not what non-cognitivists think it is, but rather lies in the fact that moral action is rational action, and in the fact that human beings are creatures with the power to recognize reasons for action and to act on them. This in no way precludes recognition of the part played by 'sentiments' such as (negatively) shame and revulsion or (positively) sympathy, self-respect, and pride in motivating human virtue. I think that David Wiggins is right often to have stressed this side of Hume's moral philosophy.[22]

---

[22] See e.g. Wiggins, 'A Sensible Subjectivism?'.

2

Natural Norms

I hope I have said enough in the previous chapter to raise doubts about the necessity and even the possibility of interpreting 'moral language' in expressivist terms. I suggested that it is 'Hume's practicality requirement' that gives such theories their undoubted attraction, and promised an account of thoughts about goodness and badness in action that would meet this requirement differently. In the following chapters of this book I shall try to make this promise good.

The central feature of my own account is that it will set the evaluation of human action in the wider contexts not only of the evaluation of other features of human life but also of evaluative judgements of the characteristics and operations of other living things. Expressivist theories have the remarkable though seldom-mentioned consequence of separating off the evaluation of human action not only from the evaluation of human sight, hearing, and bodily health but also from all evaluation of the characteristics and operations of plants and animals.[1] For it is obvious that no expressivist account will do in those other domains: we cannot think that the use of the word 'good' is to express a 'pro-attitude' in what we say about the roots of nettles or the fangs of ferocious beasts. Nowadays such evaluations are apt to be marginalized as if they were fanciful extensions of the 'proper' evaluations that express our attitudes, practical decisions, or desires. But when I was told by a certain philosopher who wanted to explain 'good' in terms of choices, that the *good* roots of trees were roots of the kind we 'should

---

[1] Here, as elsewhere, by 'animals' I mean non-human animals.

choose if we were trees', this finally confirmed my suspicion of the
kind of moral philosophy that was his. Thinking of *goodness* as emo-
tivists and prescriptivists think of it we may see as quite remarkable
that the word 'good' and its cognates can be used as it is in the
description of sub-rational living things. To be sure, almost anything
in the world can be said to be good or bad in a context that sufficiently relates it to some human concern or to the needs of a plant
or animal. But features of plants and animals have what one might
call an 'autonomous', 'intrinsic', or as I shall say 'natural' goodness
and defect that may have nothing to do with the needs or wants of
the members of any other species of living thing, and in this they are
notably different from what is found elsewhere in other things in
the world outside, as for instance rivers or storms.

Judgements of goodness and badness can have, it seems, a special
'grammar' when the subject belongs to a living thing, whether
plant, animal, or human being. This, at least, is what I argue in this
book. I think that this special category of goodness is easily over-
looked; perhaps because we make so many evaluations of other
kinds, as when we assess non-living things in the natural world,
such as soil or weather, or again assess artefacts either made by
humans as are houses and bridges, or made by animals as are the
nests of birds or beavers' dams.[2] But the goodness predicated in
these latter cases, like goodness predicated to living things when
they are evaluated in a relationship to members of species other
than their own, is what I should like to call secondary goodness. It is
in this derivative way that we can speak of the goodness of, for
example, soil or weather, as such things are related to plants, to animals, or to us. And we also ascribe this secondary goodness to living
things, as, for instance, to specimens of plants that grow as we want
them to grow, or to horses that carry us as we want to be carried,
while artefacts are often named and evaluated by the need or interest that they chiefly serve. By contrast, 'natural' goodness, as I
define it, which is attributable only to living things themselves and

---

[2] The case of artefacts is particularly interesting because they are evaluated in some
ways as living things are and in some ways not. I mention this topic only to set it aside.
See Foot, 'Goodness and Choice'.

to their parts, characteristics, and operations, is intrinsic or 'autonomous' goodness in that it depends directly on the relation of an individual to the 'life form' of its species. On barren Mars there is no natural goodness, and even secondary goodness can be attributed to things on that planet only by relating them to our own lives, or to living things existing elsewhere.

We shall of course need to consider why it is that natural goodness and defect belong only to living things and not to other objects in the world around us such as rocks and storms. What is it about living things that allows us to attribute goodness to them in this special way? Why can we not attribute natural goodness, for example, to the tributaries of rivers, when they are such as to allow a river to maintain its natural progressive pattern from upland to lake or sea?

It may be thought that the topics raised in the preceding paragraphs are of no relevance to moral philosophy, even if interesting in themselves. But this is just what I want to question. My belief is that for all the differences that there are, as we shall see, between the evaluation of plants and animals and their parts and characteristics on the one hand, and the moral evaluation of humans on the other, we shall find that these evaluations share a basic logical structure and status. I want to suggest that moral defect is a form of natural defect not as different as is generally supposed from defect in sub-rational living things. So this is what I shall go on to argue, after a discussion of 'natural goodness' as it is found in sub-rational living things.

Firstly, therefore, I shall explore natural goodness in plants and in animals other than human beings. For help I shall turn to a paper published by Michael Thompson: a paper I admire very much.

Michael Thompson's subject in this paper, which is called 'The Representation of Life', is the description of living things. His thesis is that to understand certain distinctive ways in which we describe individual organisms, we must recognize the logical dependence of these descriptions on the nature of the species to which the individual belongs. Species-dependence is his leitmotif. For this reason he concerns himself with propositions of the form 'S's are F' or 'The S is F', where 'S' holds a place for the name of a species (or 'life form' as he is ready to say for the sake of those who want to give 'species' a technical definition) and 'F' a place for a predicate; so that a representative sentence would be 'Rabbits are herbivores' or 'The rabbit is a herbivore'. He contrasts the logical form of the sentences

>   S's are F   (Rabbits are herbivores)
>   S's do V   (Rabbits eat grass)

with

>   N.N. is F   (Mrs Muff is a rabbit)
>   N.N. is doing V   (Mrs Muff is eating grass).

He points out, referring back to an early article by Elizabeth Anscombe, a peculiarity of the *logical form* of the first pair of sentences: that they are logically unquantifiable.[3] They do not speak of an individual rabbit, though the same verbal form can of course be used with that reference, as when the conjurer says to his wife 'The rabbit does not look well.' Nor, of course, do the propositions that interest Michael Thompson predicate something of every member of the species: 'Cats are four-legged but Tibbles may have only three.' Elizabeth Anscombe's original example concerned the number of teeth that human beings have—which is 32, though most human beings have lost quite a few and some never had the full complement. It is arguable that if 'The S is F' (understood in this way) is true then at least some S's must be F. But even if this is so, 'Some S's are F' is clearly not the whole of what such a proposition asserts. Thompson speaks in this context of a 'natural-history account' of the life form or species: of how creatures of this kind live. And he points out, as part of his insistence on the way in which descriptions of individuals depend on the species to which they belong, that without this reference, 'life activities' such as eating or reproducing cannot even be identified in an individual. Eating, for instance, is essentially, conceptually, related to nourishment, and could not be conclusively identified by a story about the taking in, crushing, transforming, and spewing out of substances since, for all that, its purpose might be not the maintenance of tissue but, say, skunk-like defence. Mitosis occurs in amoebae and human beings, and is given

---

[3] Anscombe, 'Modern Moral Philosophy', in *Collected Philosophical Papers*, iii. 38.

a uniform description in textbooks: in the first, however, it is reproduction of an individual organism, but in the second not.[4]

Thompson also points out peculiarities of the time references
found within such propositions. It is said for instance that certain
animals mate at a certain time of the year, and give birth, or lay eggs,
so many weeks or months later; but this is 'typically a matter of
before and after—"in the spring", "in the fall" . . . and not of now
and then . . . and when I was young and so forth'.[5] Natural-history
sentences, which Thompson also calls 'Aristotelian categoricals',
speak of the life cycle of individuals of a given species.[6] In one way,
therefore, this is the time-span with which they have to do. In
another way, however, a longer time reference is needed, since we
must speak of *reproduction*, and the characteristics of a single individual cannot determine what will count as *another of the same*.

It will no doubt be objected here that reproduction is in fact not
fixed, since species themselves are subject to change. This is of
course important, and it means that Aristotelian categoricals must
take account of sub-species adapted to local conditions. The history
of a species is not, however, the subject with which Aristotelian categoricals deal. Their truth is truth about a species at a given historical time, and it is only the relative stability of at least the most
general features of the different species of living things that makes
these propositions possible at all. They tell how a kind of plant or
animal, considered at a particular time and in its natural habitat,
develops, sustains itself, defends itself, and reproduces. It is only in
so far as 'stills' can be made from the moving picture of the evolution of species that we can have a natural history account of the life
of a particular kind of living thing. And it is only in so far as we have
a 'natural history account' that we can have a 'vital description' of
individuals here and now.

Let us now ask how all this is relevant to the normative judgements that we make about plants and animals when we say, for
instance, that a plant in our garden is diseased, or not growing properly, or that a certain lioness is a neglectful parent, or a particular

---

[4] Thompson, 'The Representation of Life', 272–3.
[5] Ibid. 282.   [6] Ibid. 267.

rabbit not as reproductive as a rabbit should be. Thompson suggests
that the relation between the Aristotelian categorical and the evaluative assessment is very close indeed. In fact, he says that if we have
a true natural-history proposition to the effect that S's are F, then if
a certain individual S—the individual here and now or then and
there—is not F it is therefore not as it should be, but rather weak,
diseased, or in some other way defective.[7] The evaluative assessment is the product of propositions of the two logically different
kinds.

Essentially, I think that Thompson is right about this, although I
seem to see a gap in his account of Aristotelian categoricals that has
to be filled in here. For I think he has not said enough to isolate the
kind of proposition that will yield evaluations of individual organisms. His talk of 'natural-history propositions' was perhaps mislead-
ing in that it did not explicitly separate out what I would like to call
the teleological from the non-teleological attachment of predicates
to a subject term that is the name of a species. Consider, for instance,
a sentence such as 'The blue tit has a round blue patch on its head.'
This is superficially like 'The male peacock has a brightly coloured
tail', but in a way of course it is not. For, on the assumption that
colour of head plays no part in the life of the blue tit, it is in this
respect quite unlike the colour of the male peacock's tail: there
would be nothing wrong with the blue tit in my garden *in that* it had
a drab-coloured head; and the peculiarity might or might not
accompany a defect. So how are we to distinguish these two types of
propositions? Or how, again, are we to distinguish the case of leaves
rustling when it is windy from that of flowers opening when the sun
comes out? It is natural to say that the rustling of its leaves plays no
part in the life of a tree, whereas pollination is gained by a display of
scent and colours in sunshine. But then we must ask what we mean
by 'playing a part in the life' of a living thing. What counts as 'its life'
in this context? And what is 'playing a part'?

There emerges here the special link, mentioned but not explored
by Thompson, between his 'Aristotelian categoricals' and teleology
in living things. Aristotelian categoricals are propositions having to

---

[7] Ibid. 295.

do with the way that certain features appear or that certain things are done in organisms of a given species either by the whole organism or by their characteristics or parts. But, speaking now for myself rather than for Thompson, I should say that to obtain the connection between Aristotelian categoricals and evaluation another move must be made. I should say that in plants and non-human animals these things all have to do, directly or indirectly, with self-maintenance, as by defence and the obtaining of nourishment, or with the reproduction of the individual, as by the building of nests. This is 'the life' characteristic of the kind of animal with which the categoricals here have to do. What 'plays a part' in this life is that which is causally and teleologically related to it, as putting out roots is related to obtaining nourishment, and attracting insects is related to reproduction in plants.[8]

We start from the fact that there is a basis for the Aristotelian categorical that does not come from the counting of heads. What is this basis? In what was said about the blue tits and the peacocks it was suggested that some but not all general propositions about a species have to do with the teleology of living things of this kind. There is an Aristotelian categorical about the species *peacock* to the effect that the male peacock displays his brilliant tail *in order to* attract a female during the mating season. The display serves this purpose. Let us call such language, purposive language. But be careful here! Where something that S's do is, in this sense, purposive we should beware of slipping over into saying of an individual S that it *has* this purpose when it does this thing. Plants grow upwards in order to get to the light, but it is fanciful to say that that is what my honeysuckle is trying to do or that that is 'its end'. Migrating birds flying off in order to reach the southern insects do not *have* this as their end or purpose even though it could be said to be the end or purpose of the operation.[9] What is crucial to all teleological propositions is the

---

[8] It is obvious that the causality here is that of necessary rather than sufficient conditions: the hazards of nature and the existence of the food chain mean that most, even healthy, members of most species of animals are unlikely to live long.

[9] It is only rarely that we can say of an individual animal that it is *trying* to do something or other, and perhaps only where it has a repertoire of ways of achieving an 'end' closely connected with these bits of behaviour, as when a dog tries to get out of a shed in which it has been confined.

expectation of an answer to the question 'What part does it play in the life cycle of things of the species S?' In other words, 'What is its function?' or 'What good does it do?'[10]

Philosophers are sometimes afraid of recognizing teleological language, thinking it must be something left over from a world-view in which all nature was seen as reflecting the will of the deity.[11] But Thompson is surely right to say

Natural-teleological judgements may . . . be said to organize the elements of a natural history; they articulate the relations of dependence among the various elements and aspects and phases of a given kind of life.

And so . . . even if the Divine Mind *were* to bring a certain life-form into being 'with a view to' securing an abundance of pink fur along the shores of the Monongahela, this would have no effect on the natural-teleological description of that form of life.[12]

What, then, determines the truth of the teleological propositions of the non-quantifiable form that meet Thompson's conditions? We start from the fact that it is the particular life form of a species of plant or animal that determines how an individual plant or animal should be: the Aristotelian categoricals give the 'how' of what happens in the life cycle of that species. And all the truths about what this or that characteristic does, what its purpose or point is, and in

---

[10] It is imperative that the word 'function' as used here is not confused with its use in evolutionary biology, where, as Simon Blackburn has put it in the *Oxford Dictionary of Philosophy*, 'the function of a feature of an organism is frequently defined as that role it plays which has been responsible for its genetic success and evolution' (149–50). Features that are functional in this sense are what Dawkins, for instance, calls 'adaptations', when he defines an adaptation both historically and as 'approximately an attribute of an organism that is "good for something"' (*The Extended Phenotype*, 290). In such contexts it is supposed to make sense to speak of the good of a species, as if a species were itself a gradually developing, one-off organism, whose life might stretch for millions of years. Perhaps the extinction of a species is imagined as a kind of death, and therefore as if it were an evil, with that which makes for its continuance thought of as 'for its good'! It is easy to confuse these technical uses of words such as 'function' and 'good' with their everyday uses, but the meanings are distinct. To say that some feature of a living thing is an adaptation is to place it in the history of a species. To say that it has a function is to say that it has a certain place in the life of the individuals that belong to that species at a certain time.

[11] Thompson, 'The Representation of Life', 293–4. See also Lawrence, 'Reflection, Practice and Ethical Scepticism', section VI, 2.

[12] Thompson, 'The Representation of Life', 294.

suitable cases its function, must be related to this life cycle. The way an individual *should be* is determined by what is needed for development, self-maintenance, and reproduction: in most species involving defence, and in some the rearing of the young.[13]

We could say, therefore, that part of what distinguishes an Aristotelian categorical from a mere statistical proposition about some or most or all the members of a kind of living thing is the fact that it relates to the teleology of the species. It speaks, directly or indirectly, about the way life functions such as eating and growing and defending itself come about in a species of a certain conformation, belonging in a certain kind of habitat. This is why the noise made by the rustling of leaves is irrelevant in this context while the development of roots is not. And this is why Aristotelian categoricals are able to describe norms rather than statistical normalities. It *matters* in the reproductive life of the peacock that the tail should be brightly coloured, whereas our assumption has been that the blue on the head of the blue tit plays no part in what here counts as 'its life'. And this is why the absence of one would itself be a defect in an individual whereas that of the other would not.

Thus, evaluation of an individual living thing in its own right, with no reference to our interests or desires, is possible where there is intersection of two types of propositions: on the one hand, Aristotelian categoricals (life-form descriptions relating to the species), and on the other, propositions about particular individuals that are the subject of evaluation.

It will be useful to remind ourselves at this point of the elements that came to light in the earlier discussion of 'good' and 'bad' as applied to characteristics and operations of plants and animals.

(a) There was the life cycle, which in those cases consisted roughly of self-maintenance and reproduction.
(b) There was the set of propositions saying *how* for a certain species this was achieved: how nourishment was

[13] In most cases we speak of what each member of the species needs to be and to do in order that *it* should flourish. But of course what is needed may be needed in a group, like cooperation in a pack, or obedience to a leader, and what a member of the species is or does may advantage others rather than himself.

obtained, how development took place, what defences
were available, and how reproduction was secured.

(c) From all this, *norms* were derived, requiring, for instance, a
certain degree of swiftness in the deer, night vision in the
owl, and cooperative hunting in the wolf.

(d) By the application of these norms to an individual member of the relevant species it (this individual) was judged
to be as it should be or, by contrast, to a lesser or greater
degree defective in a certain respect.

There are here many details that are not germane to the aim of
this book. But something more must be said about the way in which
Aristotelian categoricals about the 'how and what' of the life cycle
determine normative assessments of individual living things in the
here and now or there and then of historical place and time.

As illustration let us consider the Aristotelian categorical stating
that the deer is an animal whose form of defence is flight. From this
we know that it is a defect, a weakness, in an individual deer if it is
slow of foot. Swiftness, as opposed to fierceness or camouflage, is
what fits it to escape from its predators. But two remarks must be
added about this. In the first place, swiftness does no more than *fit* it
to survive: in some circumstances even the greatest speed possible
for this type of animal would not be enough. Moreover, by chance it
may sometimes be that the fastest deer fleeing from one predator is
the very one that gets caught in a trap.[14] Secondly, what is excellence, and what defect, is relative to the natural habitat of the
species. Even in a zoo a fleeing animal like a deer that cannot run
well is so far forth defective and not as it should be, in spite of the
fact that, as this particular individual is by chance placed, this may
be no disadvantage for defence or feeding or mating or rearing the
young.

A further consideration, when we are describing the life form of
certain animals, is that they live cooperatively. The swiftness of a
deer fits it to preserve its own life by evading a predator. And the
night vision of the owl is something it needs if *it* is to survive and

[14] As it may be the skilful archer who fails to hit a target in the presence of a freak
gust of wind.

rear its young. The fact is, however, that while there are many examples that are like this in the life of animals, there are also what we could call 'other-regarding' goodnesses and defects in their case. Take, for instance, the dance of the honey bee which tells other bees of a source of food. No doubt an individual bee that does not dance does not itself suffer from its delinquency, but *ipso facto* because it does not dance, there is something wrong with it, because of the part that dancing plays in the life of this species of bee. Similarly, cooperation is something on which good hangs in the life of the wolf, and the free-riding wolf is not behaving as it should. Such facts will be relevant when we come to consider analogies and disanalogies between the 'life forms' of animals and human beings. Peter Geach said in his book on *The Virtues* that 'Men need virtues as bees need stings', deliberately allowing for the other-regarding aspect of virtues such as justice and charity.[15] The way Geach made his point is perhaps confusing, and I should prefer to say that virtues play a necessary part in the life of human beings as do stings in the life of bees. For of course we cannot say that individual bees 'need to sting', as if they themselves would suffer if they did not. Similarly, if we imagine a species of monkeys which groom each other but not themselves, and which are not rewarded for their grooming, it would be confusing to say of them 'These monkeys need to groom'. That way of putting it might give a picture of anxious little monkeys restless until they could find some grooming to do!

Let us now turn from these remarks about the different forms that Aristotelian categoricals can take in plants and animals and sum up what has emerged about the natural norms existing, independently of human desires or interests, in this domain. We have seen that natural goodness and defect in the domain of plants and animals depends essentially on the form of life of the species to which an individual belongs. Pliability is good in a reed though a defect in an oak. (When the wind blew hard, La Fontaine's boastful oak tree was put to shame by a reed.) And an explorer would have been wrong if, meeting his first tortoise, he had marked it down for lack of speed. A strength or a weakness in a living thing cannot be

[15] Geach, *The Virtues*, 17.

identified in the same way as, say, hardness or softness in a rock. *Goodness* in plants and animals nests in an interlocking set of general concepts such as *species, life, death, reproduction,* and *nourishment,* together with less general—we might say local—ideas such as that of *fruiting, eating,* or *fleeing.* Moreover, we notice that the use of such words in such contexts is literal here, but most often fanciful or poetical when used outside the domain of living things. Nor did we need to draw on descriptions of specifically human life as if the language had to be transferred from there to be understood. Some intelligent Martians who themselves did not think in terms of goodness and badness might (even if landing in the rain forest and knowing nothing of humans) realize that the plants and animals on earth could be described in propositions with a special logical form, and come themselves to talk about the newly met living things as we do. They would rightly see the existence of this different order of things in the world as an extremely interesting ontological fact, allowing them to invent and deploy a range of concepts that they did not have before.

So far nothing has been said about primary goodness in human beings, and it is crucial to my project that there should be no cheating—no smuggling in—but rather a fresh start, when we try to see how goodness is determined for sight, locomotion, and so on in human beings, never mind for such things as character, action, and will that belong exclusively to human life. But we should notice that in the description of natural goodness in plant and animal life we have been talking about normative judgements of goodness and defect that, even here, would naturally be called 'evaluative'. If a philosopher says that 'normative' language is something different from this kind of talk, he or she may be thinking that *real* norms are something 'endorsed', though I hope that the arguments of the previous chapter may have done something to raise doubts about whether we really know what this means.[16] In any case, the norms that we have been talking about so far have been explained in terms

---

[16] Did the Brooklyn politician of Chapter 1 'endorse' the norm that he recognized when he said that what was *really* difficult was to stand up day after day for what was wrong?

of *facts* about things belonging to the natural world. We have not had to think that in evaluations of non-human living things our use of 'good' has to be explained in terms of 'commendation' or any other 'speech act', nor as the expression of any psychological state. The main thesis of this book is that propositions about goodness and defect in a human being—even those that have to do with goodness of character and action—are not to be understood in such psychological terms. In describing my view, Thompson rightly said that I saw vice as a form of natural defect, and I have therefore used a corresponding wording in the title of this book.[17]

I should be the first, however, to admit that appearances are against my thesis. For how could there be a human life form that played the same logical role in the determination of goodness here as the equivalent in the case of plants and animals? There will surely be objection to the idea that a natural form of life characteristic of humankind could determine what you or I *ought* to do. What does it matter to me *what species* I belong to? Should we not protest on behalf of individuality and creativity against bringing in the human species when asking what I myself—this particular person—should do?

My final task will be to examine such protests on behalf of human freedom and individuality. But next we must see how Thompson's schema might look if applied to human life.

---

[17] 'The Representation of Life', 296.

3

Transition to Human Beings

In the previous chapter I described the evaluation of properties and operations of plants and of animals considered in their own right, without reference to what we might desire of them or the use they might be to members of other species of living things; so it was about what I call 'natural' excellence and defect. I wrote about goodness and badness, and therefore about evaluation in its most general form; but we might equally have been thinking in terms of, say, strength and weakness or health and disease, or again about an individual plant or animal being or not being as it should be, or ought to be, in this respect or that.

Let us call the conceptual patterns found there, patterns of natural normativity. The next question is whether the same structure of judgement is to be found as we move first from plants and animals to human beings, and then from the evaluation of human characteristics and operations in general to the special subject of goodness of the will.

The idea that any features and operations of humans could be evaluated in the same way as those of plants and animals may provoke instant opposition. For to say that this is possible is to imply that some at least of our judgements of goodness and badness in human beings are given truth or falsity by the conditions of human life. And even if it is allowed that certain evaluations of this kind are possible—those vaguely thought of perhaps as 'merely biological'—there is bound to be scepticism about the possibility that 'moral evaluation' could be like this. Surely, it will be urged, we must start afresh when thinking about the subject of moral philosophy. I believe, however, that this is only partly true. Those who insist on the fresh start probably think that it is true because the core meaning of a word such as 'good' when used 'in moral judgement' must have to do with the expression of pro-attitudes or feelings, or again, with the performance of 'speech acts' such as commendation or commitment. But that way of trying to give an account of the meaning of 'good' in so-called 'moral contexts' was just what was criticized in the opening chapter of this book. I wrote it because I knew that I needed to attack that preconception in order to get so much as a hearing for the thought that there is *no change in the meaning of 'good' between the word as it appears in 'good roots' and as it appears in 'good dispositions of the human will'.*

For my own part I do not of course deny that between the evaluation of the roots of plants and of the actions and desires of human beings there is a change of characteristic context and purpose. We interest ourselves in the roots of plants at the garden centre, whereas interest in the goodness of actions has rather to do with the choice of lives, the education of children, or with decisions of social policy. But the belief that the word 'good' must *mean* something different in the former and the latter is, I think, simply a prejudice coming from the type of ethical theory that has dominated analytic philosophy in the past half-century.

Let us therefore keep an open mind about the way in which we may or may not need a fresh start when broaching the subject of goodness and defect in the human will. Human beings can be judged better or worse in many other ways as well, and we should now see whether natural normativity is in general the order of the day, or whether we have to abandon the schema as soon as we make the transition to the evaluation of rational beings such as ourselves.

After this transition, what differences and similarities do we find? With the change of subject there will of course be a great increase in the number of respects in which evaluation is possible, if only because human lives contain so many and such diverse activities: because human beings do so many different kinds of things. This variety is not, however, in itself what is most interesting from the philosopher's point of view, given that as philosophers we want to understand the *conceptual structure* of evaluation rather than details of the buzz and bloom of the animate world. So we shall want to discover not what goodness *is* in the case of, say, the activity of housebuilding over against the building of nests, but rather what goodness in performance of these and other activities may have to do with the manner of living and the good of our own species.

The question is, therefore, whether characteristics of humans can be evaluated in relation to the part they play in human life, according to the schema of natural normativity that we found in the case of plants and animals. In favour of this there is the fact that a certain network of interrelated concepts such as *function* and *purpose* is found where there is evaluation of all kinds of living things, including human beings. It is possible, of course, that the meaning of words such as 'function' or 'purpose' should diverge when used in speaking on the one hand of characteristics and operations of plants and animals and on the other of those of human beings. But it seems significant that there is a special *form* of explanation—teleological explanation—to which the idea of function and purpose is related in each case.

If we ask either with regard to a plant or to an animal *why* it does a certain thing or has a certain characteristic, we are satisfied with an answer that places this operation in the life of that species.[1] Moreover, if we consider the concepts involved we should be surprised to be told that there is no common meaning or shared logical structure between evaluations of botanical and zoological subjects. The common structure of evaluation seems unaffected by the radical difference between the two. Animals operate very differently from plants, because perception plays a large part in the way that they gain nourishment, defend themselves, and reproduce. Yet there is no reason offhand to suppose that the word 'function' has a different meaning in a sentence about the function of the spreading of a peacock's tail and in one that speaks of the opening of a flower in

---

[1] We are not then interpreting it as a historical question, as 'proper function' is interpreted, for instance, by Ruth Millikan in *Language, Thought, and Other Biological Categories*, chapter 1, and as 'function' would generally be interpreted in evolutionary biology. As David Wiggins says in Postscript 4 in *Needs, Values, Truth*, 353, 'we really need to describe what morality *has become*, a question on which evolutionary theory casts no particular light'.

sunlight. There seems to be identity in the general structure of such explanations throughout the sub-rational world, in spite of the differences appearing in a range of subsidiary concepts. It is true, for example, that an answer to a 'Why?' question about an animal may be in terms of appetite and therefore not just about what it needs but also about what it wants: even about what it 'tries to do'. Since plants do not have desires or appetites, no feature or operation in a plant can be explained by what it wants, and although we sometimes say that a plant is 'trying to get to the light', this must be recognized as a fanciful use of the words. Yet we find, as already suggested, the same structural terminology as of goodness or defect relating to parts, characteristics, and operations, and also terms such as 'function' and 'purpose' and expressions such as 'in order to' or 'in order that' in things as different from each other as plants and animals.

The question remains, however, as to whether once we have made the transition from sub-rational to rational beings we may not need a new theory of evaluation. Surely, my critics will say, it must be so, given the part that the life cycle of a plant or animal rightly played in Michael Thompson's account of the conceptual structure within which the evaluation of properties and operations of individual organisms had a place. For such an evaluation is based on the general relation of this kind of feature to the pattern of life that is the *good of* creatures of this species. But how could we possibly see human good in the same terms? The life cycle of a plant or animal ultimately has to do with what is involved in development, self-sustenance, and reproduction. Are we really going to suggest that human strengths and weaknesses, and even virtues and vices, are to be identified by reference to such 'biological' cycles?

This challenge, ill-conceived as it is in suggesting that the natural-history account of human beings could be explained in terms of a merely animal life, raises a most important and difficult topic. For it is true that in the course of describing 'natural goodness' in plants and animals we have implicitly adverted to the idea of the good of a living thing as well as its goodness in various respects, and the two ideas, though related, are distinct. That this is so can be seen if we think about what it means to benefit a plant or an animal. Very often, to be sure, a living thing is benefited by itself being made better, and there must be a systematic connection between natural goodness and benefit—whether reflexive or other-related as in the case of the stinging bees. But it does not follow that benefit of either kind follows goodness whatever circumstance an individual happens to be in. In our earlier example it was the swiftest deer, ahead of the others, that fell into the hunter's trap; and the properly acting bee that stings a gardener may well bring about the destruction of the nest.

Whether an individual plant or animal actually succeeds in living the life that it is its good to live depends on chance as well as on its own qualities. But its own goodness or defect is conceptually determined by the interaction of natural habitat and natural (species-general) 'strategies' for survival and reproduction. What conceptually determines goodness in a feature or operation is the relation, for the species, of that feature or operation to survival and reproduction, because it is in that that good lies in the botanical and zoological worlds. At that point questions of 'How?' and 'Why?' and 'What for?' come to an end. But clearly this is not true when we come to human beings.

Take reproduction, for instance. Lack of capacity to reproduce is a defect in a human being. But choice of childlessness and even celibacy is not thereby shown to be defective choice, because human good is not the same as plant or animal good. The bearing and rearing of children is not an ultimate good in human life, because other elements of good such as the demands of work to be done may give a man or woman reason to renounce family life. And the great (if often troubling) good of having children has to do with the love and ambition of parents for children, the special role of grandparents, and many other things that simply do not belong to animal life.

Moreover, the good of survival itself is something more complex for human beings than for animals; even for the animals closest to us. The human desire to live is, of course, instinctual, but it often also has to do with a desperate hope that something may yet turn out well in the future. And it seems that the preciousness of the unique memories that each person has is part of what he or she may cling to even in the most terrible of circumstances. In other words, the teleological story goes beyond a reference to survival itself.

The idea of human good is deeply problematic. One may be inclined to think of it as happiness, but much would have to be said before that could be so understood as to be true, and I shall discuss this in a later chapter. Here I want only to recall that Wittgenstein famously said on his deathbed, 'Tell them I have had a wonderful life.' The example should teach us not to be too ready to speak of every good life as 'a happy life': Wittgenstein surely did not have a happy life, being too tormented and self-critical for that.

Thus the idea of a good life for a human being, and the question of its relation to happiness, is each deeply problematic. And, moreover, there is so much diversity in human beings and human cultures that the schema of natural normativity may seem to be inapplicable from the start. Nevertheless, for all the diversities of human life, it is possible to give some quite general account of human necessities, that is, of what is quite generally needed for human good, if only by starting from the negative idea of human deprivation. For then we see at once that human good depends on many characteristics and capacities that are not needed even by animals, never mind by plants. There are, for instance, physical properties such as the kind of larynx that allows of the myriad sounds that make up human language, as well as the kind of hearing that can distinguish them. Moreover, human beings need the mental capacity for learning language; they also need powers of imagination that allow them to understand stories, to join in songs and dances—and to laugh at jokes. Without such things human beings may survive and reproduce themselves, but they are deprived. And what could be more natural than to say on this account that we have introduced the subject of possible human defects; calling them 'natural defects' as we used these terms in the discussion of plant and animal life?

We can see, moreover, that, as with animals, some defects have as we might say 'a reflexive role', in that the deprivation comes primarily to the defective individual; but that there are some that chiefly or at least most directly affect other people. We might think here, for instance, of the failure of maternal affection, or of (non-iterated) 'prisoner's dilemma' cases where each person gains from the action of others but loses through his own.[2] The way of solving the dilemma, however we should understand its details, depends on our human way of thinking. We act within a language that allows us to say 'I owe it to him' or 'I suppose I should play my part' (as we nowadays think, for instance, of taking a bus rather than a car, to reduce traffic on the road, knowing that we ourselves may need to get somewhere urgently by car some other time). There are also human enjoyments such as songs and ceremonials that need cooperative participation. And, further, human societies depend on especially talented individuals playing special roles in a society's life. As some species of animals need a lookout, or as herds of elephants need an old she-elephant to lead them to a watering hole, so human societies need leaders, explorers, and artists. Failure to perform a special role can here be a defect in a man or woman who is not ready to contribute what he or she alone—or best—can give. There is also something wrong with the rest of us if we do not support those of genius, or even special talent, in their work.

In spite of the diversity of human goods—the elements that can make up good human lives—it is therefore possible that the concept of a good human life plays the same part in determining goodness of human characteristics and operations that the concept of flourishing plays in the determination of goodness in plants and animals. So far the conceptual structure seems to be intact. Nor is there any reason to think that it could not be in place even in the evaluations that are nowadays spoken of as the special domain of morality. This special domain—and more generally that of goodness of the will—will be discussed in detail in the next two chapters. But if we ask whether Geach was right to say that human beings need virtues as bees need stings (see Chapter 2), the answer is surely that he was. Men and women need to be industrious and tenacious of purpose not only so as to be able to house, clothe, and feed themselves, but also to pursue human ends having to do with love and friendship. They need the ability to form family ties, friendships, and special relations with neighbours. They also need codes of conduct. And how could they

[2] For discussions of the 'prisoner's dilemma' see Parfit, *Reasons and Persons,* chapter IV, and Gauthier, *Morals by Agreement,* passim.

have all these things without virtues such as loyalty, fairness, kindness, and in certain circumstances obedience?

Why then should there be surprise at the suggestion that the status of certain dispositions as virtues should be determined by quite general facts about human beings? But let us see how in a particular case this would work out. Let us take a longer look at Elizabeth Anscombe's paper in which she describes how it might be shown that someone acted badly in breaking a promise or other kind of contract.[3] In the essay 'On Promising and its Justice' to which I referred in Chapter 1 she remarks that much human good hangs on the possibility of one person being able to bind another's will by something in the nature of a promise or other contract. One can see that this is true. Any exchange of goods or services above the most primitive level of direct simultaneous exchange depends on the carrying out of tacit or explicit understandings of which keeping a promise is one specific form. And it is easy to see how much good hangs on the trustworthiness involved if one thinks, for instance, of the long dependency of the human young and what it means to parents to be able to rely on a promise securing the future of their children in case of their death. It would be different if human beings were different, and could bind the wills of others through some kind of future-related mind-control device. But we have not got such powers, any more than animals who depend on cooperative hunting have the power of catching their prey as tigers do, by solitary stalk and pounce.

Anscombe stresses this human incapacity, for she asks:

What ways are there of getting human beings to do things? You can make a man fall over by pushing him; you cannot usefully make his hand write a letter or mix concrete by pushing. . . . You can order him to do what you want, and if you have authority he will perhaps obey you. Again if you have power to hurt him or help him according as he disregards or obeys your orders, or if he loves you so as to accord with your requests, you have a way of getting him to do things. However, few people have authority over everyone they need to get to do things, and few people either have power to hurt or help others without damage to themselves or command affection from

---

[3] She was not, of course, suggesting that it is always wrong to break a promise, but saying why, when it is so, it is.

others to such an extent as to be able to get them to do the things they need others to do.[4]

Anscombe believes that such considerations show that to break a promise is, in the absence of special circumstances, to act badly. The demonstration depends on an identification of elements of human good together with the story of what creatures of the human species can and cannot do. We see here the interaction of what Anscombe calls 'Aristotelian necessities' with Thompson's 'Aristotelian categoricals'. Aristotelian necessity is the necessity of that on which good hangs, and Anscombe points out that it was in just this sense that wartime posters challenged would-be travellers with the question 'Is your journey really necessary?'[5] In this same sense, she says, it is 'necessary' in many circumstances that human beings should be able to bind each other's wills. But the demonstration also relies on considerations about what human beings do, and do not, have in their repertoire that plays so large a part in determining their natural-history story.

This was the method of derivation that Michael Thompson was using in discussing goodness and defect in plants and animals, and he of course emphasizes his debt to Anscombe. Intending to follow Thompson, I offer the following botanical example for comparison. We are, let us suppose, evaluating the roots of a particular oak tree, saying perhaps that it has good roots because they are as sturdy and deep as an oak's roots should be. Had its roots been spindly and all near the surface they would have been bad roots; but as it is they are good. Oak trees need to stay upright because, unlike creeping plants, they have no possibility of life on the ground, and they are tall heavy trees. Therefore oaks need to have deep sturdy roots: there is something wrong with them if they do not, and this is how the normative proposition can be derived. The good of the oak is its individual and reproductive life cycle, and what is necessary for this is an Aristotelian necessity in its case. Since it cannot bend like a reed in the wind, an oak that is as an oak should be is one that has deep and sturdy roots.

---

[4] Anscombe, 'On Promising and its Justice', in *Collected Philosophical Papers*, iii. 18.
[5] Ibid. 15.

Thus the structure of the derivation is the same whether we derive an evaluation of the roots of a particular tree or the action of a particular human being. The meaning of the words 'good' and 'bad' is not different when used of features of plants on the one hand and humans on the other, but is rather the same as applied, in judgements of natural goodness and defect, in the case of all living things.

Something more needs, however, to be said about promise-keeping. For the derivation might (plausibly though wrongly) be thought to be of a utilitarian tenor, and thus open to the objection that in rare cases where it could be broken with the slightest risk of harm or annoyance to anyone, a promise would be without moral force. It might of course be said that as a recognized institution this would not be as useful as our own, and that one should therefore be careful not to weaken confidence in what we have. Yet this seems not to be the whole point, as the following real-life example shows.

In Kropotkin's *Memoirs of a Revolutionist* there appears the following tale. Mikluko-Maklay, a well-known geographer and anthropologist, had been sent out from Russia in the 1870s or 1880s to study the indigenous peoples of the Malayan archipelago. Kropotkin says:

[H]e had with him a native who had entered into his service on the express condition of never being photographed. The natives, as everyone knows, consider that something is taken out of them when their likeness is taken by photography. One day when the native was fast asleep, Maklay, who was collecting anthropological materials, confessed that he was awfully tempted to photograph his native, the more so as he was a typical representative of his tribe and would never have known that he had been photographed. But he remembered his agreement and refrained.[6]

This example allows us to confront the problem of the wrongness of breaking a particular promise, cut off from thoughts about the harm that might on a particular occasion result from breaking it. Maklay would have been justified in thinking that *it wouldn't do any harm* if he took the photograph. The promisee deeply wounded? The institution of promising weakened? Both wildly unlikely here.

---

[6] Kropotkin, *Memoirs of a Revolutionist*, 229.

The servant was fast asleep and the picture would not even have been developed until Maklay got back to Russia. No one need ever have known of the broken promise. Nevertheless Maklay would surely have acted badly had he taken the photograph. We can of course think of circumstances in which so much good hung on it that he would have been right to have done so; but there is nothing of that in Kropotkin's report. So why *should* he have kept his promise? How do *good* and *bad* come in here?

As a first attempt to answer this question one may remark that promises belong to the area of trust and of respect for others. It would have been deeply disrespectful of Maklay to take advantage of his servant, particularly as the latter saw it as so important not to be photographed.[7] And disrespect and untrustworthiness are bad human dispositions. It matters in a human community that people can trust each other, and matters even more that at some basic level humans should have mutual respect. It matters, not just what people do, but what they are.[8] This should be said, but may seem merely to introduce a different form of utilitarian defence, resting on the utility of dispositions.[9] And there is, in favour of such a theory, the difficulty in the idea that trustworthiness, never mind respect, could be turned off and on, as it were.

What is more germane to the argument of the present book is to notice that *utilitarianism never gets off the ground* in a schema such as we find in the work of Elizabeth Anscombe and Michael Thompson. For utilitarianism, like any other form of consequentialism, has as its foundation a proposition linking goodness of action in one way or

[7] I am not suggesting that there is anything wrong with an action *merely* because it goes against someone's wishes. It need not be wrong to give a lecture about a tribe who believed that a mention of their name in public would bring ruin on them. Nor is there always an objection to a deception, as Kant believed there was. As I remember Robert Adams remarking, there is nothing wrong with wearing a convincing toupee.

[8] It is one of the great advantages of the recently reawakened interest in the virtues that this subject comes to the fore. A virtue is more than a settled disposition to act in a certain way. See 1 Corinthians 13 on charity. And for an idea of the subtlety of this subject, see Macaulay's observation that Charles II was wrongly praised for his lack of vanity: for, said Macaulay, the king was not 'above' vanity but rather 'below' it, indifferent to the opinion of his fellow men because he saw each one as up for sale. Macaulay, *History of England,* i. 135.

[9] Compare Robert Adams, 'Motive Utilitarianism'.

another to the goodness of *states of affairs*.[10] *And there is no room for such a foundational proposition in the theory of natural normativity.* Where, after all, could 'good states of affairs' be appealed to in judging the natural goodness or defect in characteristics and operations of plants and animals? In evaluating the hunting skills of a tiger do I start from the proposition that it is a better state of affairs if the tiger survives than if it does not? What about pestilential creatures such as mosquitoes, to which the pattern of natural normativity also applies?

It could be argued that this only shows that I am wrong in thinking that the evaluation of human action has the same conceptual structure as the evaluation of operations in the sub-rational living world. For surely human beings, who are capable of judging which states of affairs are better and which worse, could never be right to choose to produce a worse state of affairs when they could produce a better? Mustn't they always choose the better over the worse? To this one should reply roundly that it is no doubt a truism that they *should* act as *well* as they can. And there is also no doubt often a place for an enquiry, somewhere *within* morality, for a question about which action will have the best consequences on the whole, given, for example, that the end is to relieve suffering or to see that justice is done. Such uses of propositions about good and worse states of affairs create no problems such as may have seemed to arise about Maklay's promise, or again about the idea that certain actions, such as torture, must always and everywhere be beyond the pale. It is only when we think of a judgement about good states of affairs as consequentialists do—that is, see it as foundational—that we go wrong.[11] The idea of good and better states of affairs does not belong to the basic structure of the evaluation of human action any more than to the evaluation of operations or other features of other living things. If there are any who dispute this they might return to

---

[10] For this structure, see Amartya Sen, 'Utilitarianism and Welfarism', 464–5.

[11] Thus, I am not wanting to run an everyday expression out of town: only to give it its proper place in the whole of a conceptual scheme. As an architect must distinguish a pillar that merely holds up an internal arch from one that is weight-bearing in relation to the building itself, so a philosopher must be careful not to exaggerate the structural importance of some common form of words.

Chapter 2 or to the example just given about goodness and defect in an oak. It would be ludicrous to suppose that in that description, which drew on the idea of botanical flourishing, I committed myself to the proposition that it was 'a good thing' if plants lived and 'a bad thing' if they died!

Nevertheless, we have not got to the bottom of the question of why Maklay was right to think that he should indeed have kept his promise even in circumstances such as those in which he found himself. It is not enough to say that natural goodness in humans requires dispositions and attitudes as well as particular actions. Nor is it enough to deny that the idea of a global best state of affairs plays any role in determining natural goodness as I understand it. For there are human virtues especially needed in scholarly work, as for instance love of truth, and it is up to a scholar to pursue the truth resourcefully and persistently. Isn't it therefore the case that Maklay positively *should* have obtained this photographic record, which might have contributed to anthropological knowledge and would by hypothesis have done no one any harm? For a solution to this problem I suspect that we have to look to a part of Anscombe's work on promising that I have not yet discussed: her work on what she has called 'stopping modals'.[12] I myself can go no further than to point out that when Maklay said to himself that he should not photograph his servant, his thought was dependent on a special kind of linguistic device that humans have developed for themselves. Something of its special nature appears if one contrasts keeping a promise with, say, doing what others expect one to do. It is often extremely useful for people to be able to anticipate each other's behaviour, so one might say that 'good hangs on it' and suppose that people should behave predictably. But of course this is true only where harm of a certain seriousness is actually likely to ensue, as when, by dashing across the road, a pedestrian makes an oncoming driver swerve. There is no basis for an objection to behaving in an unpredictable way except in its possible consequences. This is not true, however,

---

[12] Anscombe, 'Rules, Rights and Promises', in *Collected Philosophical Papers*, i. 100–2. See also 'On the Source of the Authority of the State', *Collected Philosophical Papers*, iii. 138–9 and 142–5.

of breaking a promise. In giving a promise one makes use of a special kind of tool invented by humans for the better conduct of their lives, creating an obligation that (although not absolute) contains in its nature an obligation that harmlessness does not annul.

In the preceding pages I have been applying an idea developed in previous chapters about the evaluation of operations and characteristics of plants and animals to human beings, showing something of how this would work out in terms of Elizabeth Anscombe's discussion of the wrongness of promise-breaking, and then, supposing that her view might be mistaken for a form of utilitarianism, explaining how radically a moral theory of natural normativity differs from any form of consequentialism.

In the chapter as a whole I have been following up the thought that when we think about the idea of an individual's *good* as opposed to its *goodness*, as we started to do in introducing the concept of benefit, human good must indeed be recognized as different from good in the world of plants or animals, where good consisted in success in the cycle of development, self-maintenance, and reproduction. Human good is *sui generis*. Nevertheless, I maintain that a common conceptual structure remains. For there is a 'natural-history story' about how human beings achieve this good as there is about how plants and animals achieve theirs. There are truths such as 'Humans make clothes and build houses' that are to be compared with 'Birds grow feathers and build nests'; but also propositions such as 'Humans establish rules of conduct and recognize rights'. To determine what is goodness and what defect of character, disposition, and choice, we must consider what human good is and how human beings live: in other words, what kind of a living thing a human being is.

4

Practical Rationality

In the previous chapter I described what I believe to be the conceptual underpinnings of the ascription of 'natural goodness', moving from plants and animals to human beings and suggesting that the same normative pattern is found in our evaluations of all three kinds of living things.

Now I come face to face with an apparently unanswerable objection, which is that human beings as rational creatures can ask why what has so far been said should have any effect on their conduct. For let us suppose that the normative pattern that I called 'natural normativity' does govern our evaluations of human beings as human beings. Suppose that human beings are defective as human beings unless they do what is needed for human good, including such things as refraining from murder and keeping promises. The sceptic will surely ask 'But what if I do not care about being a good human being?'

This is an objection to take seriously. For, after all, human beings are rational beings. It is part of the sea change that came at the point of transition from plants and animals on one side to human beings on the other that we can look critically at our own conduct and at the rules of behaviour that we are taught. The strange possibility seems even to arise that human beings could be as such defective in that they must sometimes either act badly, for example, in breaking a promise, or else act irrationally in keeping it where there is no reason so to do. If this were believed to be the case, our moral sceptic would probably point triumphantly to the irrelevance of a demonstration that there was human defect in promise-breaking, murder, and so on.

This is the difficulty with which the present chapter is concerned. I must, however, object to the precise way in which it was formulated. For the question is not whether we have reason to aim at being good human beings, but rather whether we have reason to aim at those things at which a good human being must aim, as for instance good rather than harm to others, or keeping faith. The problem is about the rationality of doing what virtue demands. And it has seemed to some to be an especially difficult problem for anyone who has an objective theory of moral evaluation as I do myself.

Gary Watson, a philosopher who is himself sympathetic to moral objectivism, posed this as a difficulty for someone like myself in the form of two questions:

1. Can an objective theory really establish that being a gangster is incompatible with being a good human being?
2. If it can, can it establish an intelligible connection between [this] appraisal and what we have reason to do as individuals?[1]

I accept the challenge of answering question 1 in the affirmative, having already suggested the kind of ground on which a human being could be appraised as a bad—a defective—human being if, being a gangster, he goes in for robbery and murder. I therefore answer 'Yes' to question 1 and now move on to question 2.

First, however, I want to say more about the idea that human beings are rational creatures, in being able to act on reasons, whereas even the higher animals, in many ways so like us, are different in that they cannot act rationally or irrationally because they do not act *on* reasons as we do.

It is easy to say this, but less easy to explain what we mean. The best way to understand it is, in my view, to consider what Aquinas said on the subject. That rational choice is possible for human beings is, of course, an ancient doctrine. Aristotle spends much time in expounding the idea of choice 'on a rational principle' or *logos*.[2] And Aquinas, following Aristotle as he so often does, explains this by

---

[1] Watson, 'On the Primacy of Character', 67. He says in his footnote 25 that by 'an objective theory' he means one such as my own.

[2] See Aristotle, *Nicomachean Ethics*, Book III, chapters 2–3, 1111b4–1113a14, and Book VI *passim*.

contrasting animals and men. He says that animals, like small children, do not exercise choice (*electio*). What does he mean by this? Do
sheep not choose one patch of grass rather than another when they
move to graze in a particular part of a field? Aquinas considers this
example, and allows that such animal movements 'partake of
choice' in so far as they show 'appetitive inclination' for one thing
rather than another.[3] He even stresses the fact that animals, having
perception as plants do not, may do what they do for an appre-
hended end (*propter finem*). Nevertheless he insists that in doing
something for an end animals cannot apprehend it *as an end* (*non
cognoscunt rationem finis*). A kind of knowledge is needed even for the
'participation in the voluntary' that is possible for animals. However,
Aquinas says, 'Perfect knowledge of the end consists in not only
apprehending the thing which is the end but also in knowing it
under the aspect of end and the relation of the means to that end'
('sed etiam cognoscitur ratio finis, et proportio ejus quod ordinatur
ad finem ipsum'). And similarly he denies that animals have knowledge of the relation of means and ends *as humans do*. In a way they
can be said to have this knowledge, since they go for one thing to get
another. But here, too, Aquinas says that they do not have the *kind*
of knowledge of the relation that human beings have.[4]

There is surely something interesting and important here. But
what exactly does Aquinas mean? What does it mean to speak of
not knowing an end *as an end* or a means *as a means* to that end? It is
not, after all, that human beings see something that is their quarry
as glowing in a special way, or with 'E' for End over it like the
Hollywood sign; as if animals just saw some food and moved to eat it
whereas an extra property was visible to the human eye. We may be
inclined to think that what is 'extra' over and above the apprehending that we share with animals must be something 'mental', something 'in the mind' that accompanies every act or pursuit. But of
course the idea of such an accompaniment is simply an invention of
just the kind that Wittgenstein so often exposes in his writings on

---

[3] Aquinas, *Summa Theologica*, First Part of the Second Part, Question XIII, article 2.
[4] Ibid. Question I, article 2, and Question VI, article 2.

the mind.[5] If 'seeing an end as an end' belongs to the mind, it is not in that way that it does. We must not hope to find something extra—our awareness of the *ratio*, of an end, or of the relationship of means and end—by Lockean introspection.[6] We must rather ask, as Wittgenstein teaches us, for the wider context in which the puzzling idea belongs. Here, as elsewhere, 'the inner' stands in need of public criteria, and we should ask about the surroundings in which human awareness of ends as ends could be found, looking of course at speech as well as action.

Activities are important and will play their part in allowing us to say, of a growing child, for instance, that he or she now has the idea of having a purpose and of finding something else by which it may be fulfilled. But speech is crucial here in marking the difference between animals and humans. We know what an animal is going after only by what it does, whereas a growing child will be able to tell us. Moreover, the child learns a language that includes linguistic forms that have no counterpart even in the most intricate 'language of the beasts'. A child gradually comes to use words not only to get what it wants but also to speak about what it is going to do; and comes to understand and use the locutions by which choices are debated and actions explained, justified, and recommended. It is the use of such parts of our language, appearing for the most part in regular ways in the web of actions, that allows us to say, without appealing to a *hidden* mental 'realm', that ends and means may be 'in our minds'. It makes sense to ask what someone *thought* about the pros and cons of a particular choice because we can ask him and be given an answer. And he himself can go through arguments that have as a conclusion 'so that is what I shall do'. When we say that human beings are able to choose *on a rational ground* as no animal can, it is because human action belongs in such surroundings, and so, ultimately, because humans use language not matched by anything in animal life.[7]

---

[5] See Wittgenstein, *Philosophical Investigations*, e.g. sections 157–9, 165, 171, 305–8, 444.

[6] See Locke, *An Essay concerning Human Understanding*, Book II, chapter ix.

[7] Human beings can be described as trying to achieve objectives that are remote from what they are presently doing because they can be said to 'have such and such in

Thus what Aquinas says about animals and small children being able to have ends but not to see them as ends seems comprehensible and acceptable. And the same point could be made in terms of what is seen as good. For it can be said that while animals go for the good (thing) *that they see*, human beings go for *what they see as good*: food, for example, being the good thing that animals see and go for and that human beings are able to see as good. It is for this reason that while no animal can be said to 'know the better and choose the worse', it makes sense to describe a human being as doing this. We can, to be sure, mark hesitation in an animal that is, for instance, torn between hunger and fear; but nothing in an animal's behaviour could lead us to say that it saw that one alternative was better than another but that its action did not match its thought! The problem of *akrasia* (incontinence, or so-called weakness of will) concerns a description applying only to rational beings such as us.

Let us start, therefore, with the fact that there is this great difference between human beings and even the most intelligent of animals. Human beings not only have the power to reason about all sorts of things in a speculative way, but also the power to *see grounds* for acting in one way rather than another; and if told that they should do one thing rather than another, they can ask *why* they should. Quite early on, a child learns that a 'should' needs a ground, unlike an order, which may simply be reiterated or backed up by a threat.[8]

It is, I think, the fact that a man or a woman can question what reason he or she has for doing something that makes the comparison between the 'natural' or 'autonomous' evaluation of plants or animals and the same evaluation of human beings *qua* human beings seem at first sight so unsuitable. A human being as a rational animal will ask 'Why *should* I do that?', particularly if told that he

mind'. All that is necessary for this is an ability to tell of such an objective. The objective is what they *have in mind*, though it is not something that need be occupying space in the mind like obsessive thoughts or the thinking out of a plan. Since telling is not something that animals can do, only what is immediately related to what they are doing can be their objective in the sense of what they are trying to get or to do.

[8] See Lawrence, 'Reflection, Practice and Ethical Scepticism', 341.

should do something distasteful that seems to be for the advantage of others rather than himself. And a philosopher, even if *in propria persona* a respectable person inclined to keep his promises and pay his debts, is honour bound to carry such questioning to the limit. Must he or she not either deny that natural goodness in a human being is like that same goodness in a bee or a wolf in the way I have suggested that it is, or else dismiss the fact as of no practical importance, asking to be given reason to do what a good human being does?

It is for the sake of meeting this challenge that I shall embark, in the present chapter, on a discussion of practical rationality; asking about the nature and provenance of reasons for acting.

We shall need first of all to sort out some of the rather complex conceptual connections between statements about what an agent should do and what there is reason for him to do. So we need to separate different types of proposition in which practical 'shoulds' and reason-statements appear, and can draw here on a distinction that Donald Davidson has made familiar to us: between

1. What N should do relative to a certain consideration

and

2. What N should do 'all things considered' ('a.t.c.').[9]

In speaking of what N should do relative to a certain consideration we may think of contexts such as the following. N has a nasty fluey cold one afternoon when unfortunately he needs to deposit a cheque in his bank if he is not to be overdrawn. He deliberates thus:

1. I should go out, because I need to get that money into the bank.
2. But I should stay in, because I need to nurse my cold.

Here, given that he cannot both nurse his cold and rescue his finances, we have him saying to himself 'I should go out' and also 'I

---

[9] Davidson, 'How is Weakness of the Will Possible?', in *Essays on Actions and Events*, 21–42.

should not go out'.[10] But there is, as Davidson points out, no contra-
diction, given that the two 'shoulds' are relative to different considerations. He has reason to go out and reason not to go out. Neither
(1) nor (2) gives a final or verdictive 'should'-statement about what
it is rational to do. It may be that there are stronger reasons for, for
example, staying in than going out. Or one may have simply to
plump for one or the other.

Where there *is* something that a.t.c. one should do we may say
that one of the original 'should' statements—the one that recommended the less good alternative—is, relative to the a.t.c. judgement, 'a prima facie "should"'. But I do not like this terminology for
the following reason.

Every 'should'-statement that gives even *a* reason for φ-ing must
itself be based on a certain consideration (or considerations) that can
be quoted in answer to the question 'Why do you think that that is
a reason for φ-ing?' (After all, we do not just conjure even relative
'shoulds' out of the air, and shouldn't be allowed to get away with a
claim to 'just see' that a reason exists.) My immediate point is that
these considerations (call them reason-giving considerations) may
themselves only defeasibly give any reason for acting. Take, for
instance, the consideration that a certain man is my father, as it
might stand as evidence for the proposition that there is reason for
me to look after him in old age. No doubt the fact of being someone's offspring is usually reason-giving, and in families there are
often anguished deliberations about what, in view of this *relative*
'should', ought a.t.c. to be done. But now suppose that this man is
my father only by virtue of having raped my mother and that he
later offered her no support. It would seem a bit thick that he should
say that I had *any* reason to help him. The fact that he was my father

---

[10] He will also have to take into account any other reasons for doing one action
rather than another, since other considerations will usually have come in if only to the
ruling out of other alternatives, as for instance that he should telephone a neighbour
(whom he hardly knows) and ask him to collect the cheque and take it to the bank.
It is seldom that there would not be a way of nursing the cold and avoiding being
overdrawn *whatever was against using that method*, and when I said that he could not
both nurse the cold and avoid being overdrawn, I meant that there were no eligible
means.

was a prima-facie ground for saying that I had such a reason, but in view of all the circumstances there was actually no 'should' at all; nothing that had even to be taken into account in deliberating what to do.

I prefer, therefore, to keep the description 'prima facie "should"' for this case, and shall refer to the 'shoulds' in my original example concerning the nursing of a cold and the avoiding of an overdraft as relative 'shoulds'. There is also, however, to be considered the judgement that 'All things considered, N should φ'. For suppose we add to the previous example the fact that N finds he has a temperature of 103 degrees. Undoubtedly he has flu and if he struggles out he risks serious illness. In such a situation the only rational thing for him to do is to stay in. It is just too bad that inconveniences will follow from the fact that his account at the bank will be overdrawn. He should stay in. It is the rational thing to do. He may of course say that it is bad that he is going to be overdrawn, but this only means that it is unfortunate: something to be deplored. If he stays in, he acts as he should (final 'should') have acted, which implies that he did not act badly in so doing. He would rather have acted badly— imprudently—had he gone out in the circumstances as now described, though we can add other elements that would have made it the right thing to do, for instance by supposing that the prevention of an accident hung on his rising from his bed. In the absence of a new condition such as this, we had in our example an overriding or final 'should'.

Let us now see what this implies. It implies that there was reason for the agent to do the action named in the 'should'-proposition; but that was implied by relative 'shoulds' as well. (He had reason to go to the bank as well as reason to stay in bed.) The special characteristic of an a.t.c. or final 'should' is its conceptual connection with practical rationality, as was suggested above when we said that with a temperature of 103 degrees, the only rational thing to do was to stay in. This has important consequences. For the actions of anyone who does not φ when φ-ing is the only rational thing to do are *ipso facto defective*. It does not matter whether we say that he acts irrationally, or rather say 'acts in a way that is contrary to practical rationality'. In either case it is implied that he does not act well.

It is this 'should' that we must be concerned with when we set
out to answer Gary Watson's challenge, because his question—put
in terms of showing a reason for acting—was, of course, about practical rationality. At this point I want, therefore, to go back to consider an old article of mine that has (rightly) come in for plenty of
adverse criticism. In that article, 'Morality as a System of
Hypothetical Imperatives', I pointed out that the question of the
rationality of moral action was not settled by showing that a moral
judgement was like a Kantian categorical imperative in that its truth
did not depend on an agent's desires or interests. For this same inde-
pendence belongs to a whole range of propositions that are never
thought to have that status, such as, for instance, those detailing the
rules of a club. If someone is a member of a club he can be told that
he should not do this, that, or the other, and he cannot deny it on
the ground that this is nothing to him. The unchangeable truth of
what is said does not, however, show that there is any reason for the
agent to act as the rules prescribe. In *The Brothers Karamazov*,
Dostoevesky has Father Zosima telling how as a young man he had
abandoned a duel with an apology. When his second cried out that
it was against the rules to apologize in the middle of a duel, he
replied:

'Gentleman, is it really so extraordinary in these days to meet a man who
will acknowledge his own stupidity and apologise in public for the wrong he
has done?'
'But not in a duel,' shouted my second again.[11]

My point in bringing forward such examples was, of course, to
insist that the rationality of moral action was not in any way to be
bolstered up by the fact that the 'shoulds' they contained were independent of an agent's interests or desires. And (intransigently) I suggested that until the matter was otherwise demonstrated, we should
say that only interests or desires could give practical rationality to
moral action.

I now wonder why, given the obvious indigestibility of the idea

---

[11] John Jones gave me this example. I particularly like, and have used, his transla-
tion, from his *Dostoevsky*, 330.

that morality is indeed a system of hypothetical imperatives, I should have accepted it even for a short while. What seemed to force it on me was the sheer difficulty of showing a practical rationality that was independent of desire or interest. But why, we may ask, did these particular demonstrations, or some clever adaptation of them, seem the only possible ones to be considered by those of us who were not to be satisfied by any Kantian alternative? Why did desire and interest continue to hover as candidates? I think that their seductiveness depends for most people on a combination of two factors.

Firstly, each can *be* a genuine reason-giving factor. A desire to see the Taj Mahal can in the right circumstances make it rational to plan a trip to India and visit a travel agent; and similarly the knowledge that cigarettes are carcinogenic can rationalize giving up smoking by showing that it is in one's interest to do so.[12]

Secondly, to many philosophers each is apt to seem to have a *special*, perhaps *unique*, power to explain human action. That this is the case seems, and always seemed, to me to be merely an illusion rife among philosophers. For after all an action can be explained by all sorts of causes, as for instance (a) habit, (b) a tendency to mimic the actions of others, (c) something significant about the occasion on which one first did what one is now going to do, (d) the fact that it is substitutionally representing some other action, or (e) even something as far out as post-hypnotic suggestion. What tells us that conscience cannot explain action? Someone may give as the explanation of his action a thought about right and wrong, and it may be a true explanation, as Kropotkin clearly supposed in his story of Maklay's decision not to photograph his sleeping servant (see Chapter 3 above). So offhand we have no reason to suppose that acting as conscience demands has to be brought into a special mould, as of a belief and a 'conative state', before we can see it as a genuine explanation of what someone does. If we like, we can say

---

[12] That prudence on its own can motivate seems to me to have been demonstrated by Thomas Nagel many years ago, in *The Possibility of Altruism*, chapters V and VI. If philosophers still insist that only the presence of what they call a 'conative state' can explain an action, they are, to my mind, ignoring his lesson.

that someone whose action is explained in this way is 'wanting to do what is right'; but now we are simply expressing the agent's intention in terms of wanting, not showing the explanation as fitting a favoured mould.

The problem is not, then, to show that a belief about right and wrong can explain an action, but that a belief of such a kind can give the agent reason to do or not to do it.[13] Can it be the case that someone who does what is wrong *thereby* acts in a way that is contrary to reason? May we add considerations that are about right and wrong to the list of rationalizing considerations given above? I suggested in Chapter 1 that we can indeed do so, because one who acts badly *ipso facto* acts in a way that is contrary to practical reason. This was the view that Warren Quinn suggested, and I now want to argue for it and consider its consequences.

In his article 'Rationality and the Human Good', Quinn attacked a view of practical rationality that he called 'neo-Humean' and defined as 'one that makes the goal of practical reason the maximal satisfaction of an agent's desires and preferences, suitably corrected for the effects of misinformation, wishful thinking, and the like.'[14] He pointed out that by this account, practical reason, which would concern only the relation of means to ends, would therefore be indifferent to nastiness or even disgracefulness in an agent's purposes. And Quinn asked, in the crucial sentence of the article, *what then would be so important about practical rationality?* In effect he is pointing to our taken-for-granted, barely noticed assumption that practical rationality has the status of a kind of master virtue, in order to show that we cannot in consistency with ourselves think that the Humean account of it is true. Seeing this as a move of great originality and extreme importance, I asked myself why, if there were indeed this conceptual restraint on practical rationality, it should be supposed that there is an independent concept of it with which the requirements of moral goodness must somehow be shown to be

---

[13] Christine Korsgaard brilliantly demonstrated this in her classic article 'Scepticism about Practical Reason'. She and I agree in our opposition to internalist theories of motivation, but differ radically in our accounts of the foundations of morality.

[14] 'Rationality and the Human Good', in *Morality and Action*, 210.

consonant.[15] I see Quinn as watching us all struggling to tie a horse to the back of a cart, and suggesting 'Try it the other way round'.

This now seems to me to be the correct way of meeting the challenge that I myself issued in 'Morality as a System of Hypothetical Imperatives' and at that time despaired of meeting: namely, to show the rationality of acting, even against desire and self-interest, on a demand of morality. The argument depends on the change of direction that Quinn suggested: seeing goodness as setting a necessary condition of practical rationality and therefore as at least a part-determinant of the thing itself.[16] Nor is this a quite unfamiliar way of arguing. Many of us are willing to reject a 'present desire' theory of reasons for action because we think that someone who knowingly puts his future health at risk for a trivial pleasure is behaving foolishly, and therefore not well. Seeing his will as defective, we *therefore* say that he is doing what he has reason not to do. Being unable to fit the supposed 'reason' into some preconceived present-desire-based theory of reasons for action, we do not query whether it really is a foolish way to behave, but rather hang on to the evaluation and shape our theory of reasons accordingly. And it is exactly a generalization of this presumption about the *direction* of the argument on which I am now insisting. For what, we may ask, is so special about prudence that it alone among the virtues should be reasonably thought to relate to practical rationality in such a way?

With all this in mind I shall now return to Gary Watson's challenge to those who hold objective theories of moral judgement such as my own. It will be useful to begin by speaking about reason in general under the following headings:

(A) Reasons for acting, which we may call practical reasons.
(B) Reasons for believing, which we may call evidential or demonstrative reasons.

As philosophers, and therefore theoreticians, our job is of course to

---

[15] Later in this article Quinn gives an explicitly Aristotelian account of human good.

[16] The mathematical coherence of choices, and that they be as informed as they should, could also be requirements of practical rationality.

give the second type of reason, arguing for or against the truth of a variety of propositions that seem to involve special problems—like those, for instance, about personal identity or the existence of an external world. But among these many 'philosophical' subjects we find that of the nature of practical reasons, and in this special case we shall have to give reasons of type B for theses about reasons of type A. (This is what has been going on in the present chapter, as it was in Quinn's article.) When Gary Watson issued the challenge described on p. 53 above, he was asking a question that belongs here, since he was wanting to know whether on an objective theory of moral goodness an 'intrinsic link' could be established between moral goodness and *reasons for action*. My argument in the last few pages has been designed to show that there is such a link.

Earlier in the book, in Chapters 1–3, I gave reasons for believing propositions about natural goodness and badness in various plants, animals, and human beings; for instance, for believing that an individual oak tree with superficial, spindly roots was to be evaluated as defective, and, passing to human beings, gave reasons *of the same form* for the assertion that Maklay would have acted badly had he photographed his sleeping servant. In the latter case the immediate reason was that he had promised not to do so, and I drew on Anscombe's arguments for the assertion that, absent extenuating circumstances, to break a promise was as such to act badly. Finally, supposing that doubts might be raised about the relevance of such considerations to moral philosophy, I argued for the extension of the concept of natural normativity to human beings, even to the moral evaluation of human action and will, and so argued for what Watson regarded as an objective theory of moral judgement. In the previous pages I have turned to the problem of practical reasons, and have gone on to answer 'Yes' to his question 2.

Returning now to the beginning of the present chapter, to the sceptic who was supposed to have asked why he should do that which the good person must do, I would point out that there are two ways of understanding this question. If we understand the words 'that which a good person must do' 'transparently' (extensionally) as referring to, for example, keeping promises or refraining from murder, then our answer must consist in showing him why in doing *these things* he would act badly, and we are still in Chapters 1–3. But if his words are understood opaquely (intensionally) as referring to *bad actions* under that description, we must try to show him the conceptual connection between acting well and acting rationally; so that if he is to challenge us further, this is where the challenge must come. If the sceptic does not succeed in refuting us here, but still goes on saying that he has not been shown that there is reason for acting as a good person would act, it is no longer clear what he is asking for. To ask for a reason for acting rationally is to ask for a reason where reasons must a priori have come to an end. And if he goes on saying 'But why *should* I?', we may query the meaning of this 'should'.

No doubt what our sceptic (especially if he be a gangster) really means to insist is that we have not been able, in anything we have said, to touch his desires; and if he is a dangerous person that may be what we shall most care about. But the fact that we might hunt around for something that has a chance of affecting his actions should not be taken as giving any support to a philosophy that takes practical reasons to encompass only reasons of that kind.

5

Human Goodness

In earlier chapters I described a logical structure that belongs to the evaluation of all living things 'in their own right', or 'autonomously'; that is, where 'natural' goodness or defect is in view. I said something about differences as well as similarities in the evaluation of plants, animals, and human beings. But now, as we move in towards the subject of 'moral goodness', new specialities appear, and we see that we have a way of speaking of goodness in human beings not corresponding to anything in the other cases. I am thinking now of the thoughts expressed by sentences in which the word 'good' is joined to the name of the species itself, as when we speak of 'a good human being' or, more colloquially, 'a good person'. There is no equivalent to this in the language in which we evaluate plants and animals. Firstly, in so far as we do speak of 'a good S' in these other cases (where, incidentally, we tend rather to say 'a healthy S' or 'a good specimen of an S'), we are thinking about the plant or the animal as a whole; whereas to call someone a good human being is to evaluate him or her only in a certain respect. And as suggested in the previous chapter, this particular evaluation can only be of human beings. For to speak of a good person is to speak of an individual not in respect of his body, or of faculties such as sight and memory, but as concerns his rational will.[1]

In the present chapter I want to consider this particular case of evaluation in more detail, and it may seem that I have now reached the subject of 'moral evaluation'. But I want to show that the judgements usually considered to be the special subject of moral philoso-

---

[1] As an approximation, we may say 'will as controllable by reason'.

phy should really be seen as belonging to a wider class of evaluations of conduct with which they share a common conceptual structure. It is worth remarking that in considering *reasons for action* in the
earlier chapters we seemed to move quite naturally between the
example of someone kept in bed by flu and that of the explorer
Maklay bound by his promise to his servant. Various observations
were made about the relation between the concepts of *goodness* and
reasons with no distinction of 'non-moral' and 'moral' examples.
Was this a mistake? I shall try to show that it was not.

My own view is that it is right to see moral judgements as belonging with other evaluations that may perhaps appear not weighty
enough to merit such proximity. Thinking about reasons for action,
we saw that there is a use of the word 'should' (a practical 'should')
that implies a reason, and even an 'a.t.c.' reason for action.[2] And we
noticed that a certain kind of human goodness—call it practical
rationality—hung on the doing of that which *should* be done. But as
Elizabeth Anscombe pointed out, 'should' is 'a rather light word
with unlimited contexts of application'.

We say that 'athletes should keep in training, pregnant women watch their
weight, film stars their publicity, that one should brush one's teeth, that one
should (not) be fastidious about one's pleasures, that one should (not) tell
"necessary" lies . . .'[3]

The use of 'should' in such practical contexts tells us of a possible
defect in action, but does not itself tell us whether or not anything of
importance is involved. Anscombe shows in other places that she
regards lying as often a very serious transgression, but this could not
be said of other items in her list. A 'should not' or 'should' may
mark something very important, but often an action that it would be
merely silly to do or not to do.

How is it then that moral evaluation seems to most philosophers
nowadays to be a very special subject, that may have to be understood in terms of the expression of special mental states such as
approval, or mental acts such as endorsing? This must have something to do with the fact that these philosophers are focusing on

---

[2] This is the only case that I shall consider from now on.
[3] Anscombe, *Intention*, section 35.

evaluations which are often used in a special context, as when members of society are expressing disapproval of something others have done, and especially where the public good or the rights of a third party are involved. Use in such contexts should not, however, be taken to imply a special logical grammar. Whether or not there is one is the subject next to be explored.

Many if not most moral philosophers in modern times see their subject as having to do exclusively with relations between individuals or between an individual and society, and so with such things as obligations, duties, and charitable acts. It is for this reason that, of the four ancient cardinal virtues of justice, courage, temperance, and wisdom, only the first now seems to belong wholly to 'morality'. The other three virtues are recognized as necessary for the practice of 'morality' but are now thought of as having part of their exercise 'outside morality' in 'self-regarding' pursuits, 'moral' and 'prudential' considerations being *contrasted* in a way that was alien to Plato or Aristotle.[4] J. S. Mill, for instance, expresses this modern point of view quite explicitly, saying in his essay *On Liberty* that 'A person who shows rashness, obstinacy, self-conceit . . . who cannot restrain himself from harmful indulgences' shows faults (Mill calls them 'self-regarding faults') which 'are not properly immoralities' and while they 'may be proofs of any amount of folly . . . are only a subject of moral reprobation when they involve a breach of duty to others, for whose sake the individual is bound to have care for himself'.[5]

There is of course nothing wrong with using the word 'moral' as Mill does. It fits in with much of our everyday usage, and I do not want to involve myself in a discussion of the variations in usage found even today.[6] What concerns me is not the exact meaning of 'moral' when used as Mill used it but rather the substance, if there is any substance, of a distinction between 'moral' evaluation and the other evaluations of which he wrote in the passage just quoted.

---

[4] Gavin Lawrence is a notable exception to the generalization I have just made. See Lawrence,'The Rationality of Morality', 106.

[5] Mill, *On Liberty*, chapter IV, 134–5.

[6] I would remark, however, that Isaiah Berlin spoke in a lecture of the 'moral impact' of the Busch Quartet's recording of late Beethoven quartets.

Perhaps it will seem strange even to raise the question of substance, because there is after all a special lexicon for Mill's 'sphere of morality'. Words such as 'wicked' and 'evil' are applied to a deed such as murder but not to even the greatest act of self-destructive folly as such. Even to call an action 'wrong' outside some technical context is to imply that it is unjust, or perhaps uncharitable; that it has to do with conduct whose defect lies in what is done against other individuals or against the public good. Indeed, parts of this special 'moral' vocabulary serve the purpose of picking out special relationships in which individuals stand to other individuals or to society, as, for example, that of having rights, obligations, or duties. And some of these words such as 'wicked' and 'evil' also mark the seriousness of the subject, and the extreme reactions evoked by horrifying and revolting actions of murderers, child abusers, or torturers. The social and emotional surroundings of our use of the vocabulary of moral censure are very different from those settings in which we speak of rashness, obstinacy, imprudence, and folly. But I shall argue that there are features common to all these evaluations that may be labelled 'evaluations of the rational human will'.

What, then, are the features that such evaluations share? In the first place, they all have as their subject not physical or mental abilities, but voluntary action and purpose. This is something that is generally recognized where 'moral' evaluation is concerned. For it is obvious that not everything that humans *do* counts for or against moral goodness. No one is called a murderer because in slipping and falling on a mountainside he has killed someone. What is done involuntarily does not feature, and force, too, can take away voluntariness of movement, as in one who is blown along by the wind or carried away by strong men.[7] Moreover, we must surely count not perhaps as involuntary but as less than voluntary what is done under torture that no one could be expected to withstand.

A more difficult part of this subject opens up, however, when acting with knowledge is added to the conditions of an action's voluntariness.[8] Some examples of excuse in this area are evident enough.

---

[7] Cp. Aristotle, *Nicomachean Ethics*, Book III, chapter 1, 1110a1–34.
[8] Ibid. 1110b18–1111a20.

For a doctor might kill a patient she was treating in emergency conditions (as, for instance, when the victim was trapped halfway up a cliff), but do this only through ignorance of the patient's allergy to a standard drug. This doctor might say that sadly she had done the wrong thing; but she had perhaps acted heroically in climbing up to give help. Here we must agree with Kant that the unfortunate outcome is irrelevant to goodness of the will, and blame 'step-motherly Nature' instead.[9]

The action of the doctor in this example, though it was intentional under the description 'giving treatment', was of course not intentional under the description 'killing'—under which it could otherwise have been an immediate subject of adverse moral judgement. The example was, however, carefully chosen. For not every case of acting in ignorance is excusable in this way. Our doctor acted in an emergency, so that discovery of the allergy was ruled out. And it was implied that she gave the standard treatment, as any conscientious medic would have done.

This last remark points to the fact that lack of knowledge of what one is doing, though it 'takes away something of voluntariness', does not always excuse. For ignorance itself may be voluntary, as when, in present-day Britain, an arms dealer takes care not to enquire whether the weapons that he is shipping to one country will not be shipped on to a repressive regime. Or if he 'enquires', his conclusion may be guided by self-interest rather than by the evidence at hand: he holds a convenient opinion that does not absolve him, because it is not held, as we say, in good faith.[10] Furthermore, an agent's ignorance may be imputed to his will if, through negligence, he has not taken the trouble to find out facts that he could, and should, have known. This is a particularly interesting case, as well as one that is of everyday practical importance. There may be no moment at which this person decided not to discover the facts, or made it impossible to do so. The fault may be one of pure omission; but omission in action is a common fault, and omitting to find out

---

[9] Kant, *Foundations of the Metaphysics of Morals*, section 1.

[10] Many of the beliefs of slave owners, and of white people under South Africa's apartheid regime, must have been of this kind.

what one could and should have found out is only a special case of this. The omission may be culpable on account of some special position of responsibility held by the agent, but the practical importance of the subject of culpable ignorance does not come only from special positions of responsibility. For are there not things that most adults in countries such as Britain not only could but should know? I am thinking, for instance, of the basic principles of first aid, and procedures such as cardiac pulmonary resuscitation. To say this may seem to be going too far, given that no one can be expected to know everything that he or she might need to know in order to save a life. But such examples give a clue to the criteria by which it can be judged that most of us here not only can but also should learn about first aid. That there must be a 'should' as well as a 'could' for culpable ignorance is seen by contrasting this example with one that I remember Elizabeth Anscombe giving to illustrate the point. Suppose, she said, that an infant had been left on the doorstep of her house and had perished during the night because she had not known that it was there. It is not that she could not have known, because had it been her practice to check her doorstep every hour upon the hour through every night this child would have been saved. But of course it cannot be said that she should have done this. Nor is it difficult to see the factors that distinguish this example from that of failure to learn elementary first aid. In both cases, as it happens, the evil that could come about through ignorance is very great, and this is relevant. On the other hand, the likelihood of such knowledge being needed is very different, and so too is the cost to the agent of getting it.[11]

With these observations we have been tracing logical limits to evaluations whose subject is goodness and defect of human action considered as such. The discussion may have seemed to have to do in particular with what is nowadays called 'moral judgement' and

---

[11] The case of acting in ignorance through failure to find out what one could and should have found out is particularly interesting from the point of view of philosophy of mind. For this voluntariness is attributed to the action on account of what should have been known, and so to the agent's will *in a way that depends on evaluation itself*. The idea that voluntariness is discovered by a *causal* investigation of the operation of a faculty is hereby shown as a mistake.

was explicitly distinguished as such by Mill. Yet 'self-regarding' failings come under the heading of lack of wisdom, and the corresponding descriptions are conceptually constrained by conditions of voluntariness, as are 'moral' descriptions such as 'wicked'. No one is said to do something foolish when what he does is involuntary, as, for instance, if he falls into the sea when hit by a giant wave. And here, too, ignorance may absolve, as it absolves of imprudence those who took up smoking in the years before the link between smoking and cancer was known. But, as before, ignorance has this logical force only when it was itself not ignorance of what the agent could and should have known. An illiterate in our society who could learn to read, but does not take the trouble to do so, shows lack of wisdom. And *wisdom* is a telling concept from just this point of view because it itself implies no more knowledge and understanding than anyone of normal capacity can and should acquire in the course of an ordinary life.

A special connection with the voluntary is, then, the first of the conceptual marks of the special evaluations, picked out from others (such as speech defects) which have to do with goodnesses and defects *in* human beings but are not of the kind that I have indicated by saying that they are about goodness and defect *of the rational will*. And my present point is that their subject matter is more extensive than that picked out by Mill when he spoke of 'morality'. So there is this first reason for treating the subject of the virtues as a whole, as the ancients did.

There is, moreover, a second important feature of Mill's 'moral' evaluations that can be shown to belong to this wider class. It can be summarily described by saying that goodness or badness can come from different formal features of a single action, which may be distinguished as follows.

Firstly, goodness can come from the nature of the action itself—from what it is that is done. So, in general, an act of saving life is good in this respect, while an act of killing is bad.[12]

---

[12] I am in general following Aquinas in making these distinctions; but what he says about species and circumstances of an action is complex, and I am not trying exactly to represent his view about this. It is natural to say that circumstances often affect the goodness or badness of an action, as the circumstance that the subject has been con-

Secondly, the end for which an action is done is an independent source of goodness or badness in it. A good (even obligatory) action may be bad in that it is done for a bad end, as a blackmailer may save the life of his victim in order to continue his extortion. Or, again, a bad action may be done for a good end but one that does not justify it; as when an executor destroys a will in order to see that money goes to a poor person rather than a rich legatee. Contrast an end that does justify, like the need to destroy someone's property to stop the spread of a fire.

A third source of goodness or badness in an action lies in its relation to the agent's judgement of whether he or she is acting badly or well. Here, too, goodness or badness may be combined with either goodness or badness in either act or end. It is often supposed that the fact that someone is doing what he *thinks* right is a circumstance that annuls actual badness of act or purpose; but Aquinas (whose discussion of this topic is a wonderful piece of moral philosophy) insists that erring conscience does not excuse.[13] What Aquinas says is illustrated by a sad story of the fate of a Jewish child sent to a family in Norway in hope of safety when Prague was overrun by the Nazis. She died in Auschwitz because, after the invasion of Norway, the Norwegian family who loved the child thought that it was their duty to hand her over to the Gestapo when ordered to do so. They believed, no doubt through some sympathy with the Nazis, that this was 'the right thing to do'. The erring conscience, or as Aquinas always says, 'reason or conscience' (*ratio vel conscientia*), does not excuse.

Nevertheless, according to Aquinas, to go against one's conscience is itself a source of badness in an action, even when it tells one to do what in fact one should not do. Even an erring conscience binds, he says, because in going against conscience the will tends to an action as something evil in that reason has proposed it as evil.

victed of a crime by due process of law changes what is done in depriving him or her of liberty. And an end can also operate in this way as a circumstance, though this is not, of course, to say that even a good end will always do so. See the discussion of 'absolutism' on pp. 77–80, 114–115.

[13] See Aquinas, *Summa Theologica*, First Part of the Second Part, Question XIX, articles 5 and 6.

And surely this is right. For acting as one thinks one should not is a very radical form of badness in the will. How could a human being be acting well in doing what he or she saw as evil? Is that not as if an archer should not even aim his arrow at where the target seemed to him to be?

What, then, should the Norwegian couple have done? On Aquinas's reckoning they would have acted badly whether they had or had not given up the Jewish child. The point is that in such a situation there is no way for people *of such views* to act well, and in this example it is not unreasonable to say that they were at fault in this. They already knew that the child needed shelter from the Nazis, and that the Nazi policies were wicked was something that they could and should have recognized. It is hard, however, to believe as Aristotle and Aquinas both suggest, that errors of *principle* are never excusable. There are, after all, famously disputable matters of right and wrong.[14]

I have gone into the question of different sources of badness in action because it seems to me that the subject is seldom well treated in modern moral philosophy. So far, my examples in this section have been from the area that Mill assigned to morality. But these faults have their parallels in those that he excluded, in which self-destructiveness takes the place of cruelty to others, and indifference to one's own good that of indifference to theirs. Thus, firstly, there are generally bad acts, such as self-mutilation or suicide, whose badness need not depend on harm likely to come to anyone else.[15] Secondly, no one can act well in seeking, or carelessly incurring, even a lesser harm to himself through self-hatred or the kind of spitefulness to oneself that Dostoevsky unforgettably described in *Notes from the Underground*. Finally, here again one cannot act well in doing what, rightly *or even wrongly*, one seriously thinks that one should not do.

---

[14] See Anscombe, 'The Two Kinds of Error in Action'.

[15] Except in certain fairly rare cases, for instance of great suffering in a terminal illness, suicide is contrary to the virtue of hope. It may surprise some people that I call hope a virtue, but of course it is; in part because we are often tempted to think that all is lost when *we cannot really know that it is so*. In view of the appalling number of young suicides in our present society, I suggest that hope should be among the first of a fairy godmother's gifts at the cradle of a child.

So far, therefore, we have seen no reason to think that Mill's 'moral' evaluations should be treated differently from other evaluations concerning the human will. Nor does one appear if we continue the investigation by asking about the overall judgement in cases where there is a mixture of good and bad in cases such as those described in the previous paragraph, and where there may of course also be goodness *and* badness from 'inside' and 'outside' of Mill's specially distinguished area of morality. In our much earlier example of the foolish burglar whose action was defective in one way in that he was plying his dishonest trade and in another in that he was tarrying in front of the television set (Chapter 1), we have a double dose of badness. So we may mix and match ad lib and then ask about the result. What if different elements point evaluation in different directions? When can an action be called good in such a case? Will it, for instance, be enough for goodness that what is done is (intentionally) to save a life or bring some other kind of help to a person who needs it? This seems plausible until we think of a blackmailer saving someone from drowning only so as to be able to go on with his extortion. And what again of an action with a good end but carried out by immoral or by foolish means; or of an action that in itself perhaps *should* be done but is *thought* to be foolish or 'wrong' by the doer? Can any of these actions, containing both good and bad elements, be called good? Aquinas, whose distinctions we followed earlier, says firmly that in every one of them the actions are bad, invoking the principle that a single defect is enough for badness, while goodness must be goodness in all respects.[16]

Aquinas here sees asymmetry in the concepts of badness and goodness, which may strike one at first sight as simply wrong. Yet on reflection we observe that this is indeed part of our way of thinking. It is enough to make a house a bad house that it is either badly designed or damp, whereas neither the fact that a house is well designed nor the fact that it is dry is sufficient to make it good. Small faults are not always counted in, but a consideration of major faults and excellences works in this asymmetrical way.

[16] Aquinas, *Summa Theologica*, First Part of the Second Part, Question XVIII, article 4.

It seems, then, that an action is bad if it has badness from its kind, its end, or its contrariety to the agent's beliefs about what it is good or bad to do. So much for the negative side: we now know what is, formally speaking, sufficient for volitional defect. But what of goodness? What is sufficient for that? Again Aquinas says something that may surprise us. For he says of any individual action (that is, one individuated by the fact that it is done by a particular person at a particular date and time) that *if it is no way bad then it is good*.[17] This has also seemed evident to Anscombe.[18] I remember protest at a convivial philosophical gathering when I remarked as someone started to drink a glass of wine that he was acting well. Yet the principle 'good if not bad' is one that should be seen as unexciting and unexceptional when applied to an operation of a living thing. A plant, after all, is growing well if there is nothing wrong with its development. And we would naturally think in the same way of, for example, the movements of a human hand. If a hand is either weak or spastic, its movements are, in one or the other of these ways, defective. In the absence of any defect it will, however, be said to be good in its operation, just as a normal, healthy child will come to have what we call good balance, to walk well, to talk well, and to relate well to other children.

It may be said that we think differently about human action, and it is true that we sometimes do when it comes to picking out certain actions for special praise. But then it is important to remember that no special praise is due when a rich person contributes to charity a sum of money that he or she would not even miss; while a simple action like telling the truth in a law court, or giving honest opinion on a candidate for an academic position, may merit special praise when performed in especially difficult circumstances.[19] Under Hitler's regime, as under Stalin's, the temptation to prevaricate must have been very great indeed. And extra special goodness does not belong only to what is generally thought of as belonging to the

---

[17] Ibid. article 9.

[18] Anscombe, 'Practical Inference', 34.

[19] It is important, of course, to distinguish difficult *circumstances* from the kind of difficulty that comes from lack of virtue itself. For this distinction see Foot, 'Virtues and Vices', section II.

sphere of morality. For clearly it can be an exercise of the virtues of hope and of courage simply to struggle on rather than commit suicide in the face of great adversity. To behave with wisdom in fortunate circumstances may be nothing special, but for a single mother with small children in cramped bed and breakfast accommodation it must be very hard indeed. As a certain doctor put it,

it is easy to eat healthily . . . and to address your addiction to cigarettes *if you are not having to deal with conditions that challenge your capacity to get, intact, from one end of the day to the other.*[20]

If acting wisely rather than self-destructively in such circumstances were said to be the kind of action that should be picked out as especially good, one could go along with that.

So far, then, our conceptual analysis has seemed to favour a comparison rather than a contrast between the two classes of evaluations that I see as belonging together. One who objects to this has, however, another card to play. For he or she may insist that there is nevertheless a *logical difference* between 'moral' and 'non-moral' evaluations because, in a clash of reasons for action based on requirements of justice or charity and reasons having to do with one's own needs or desires, the former always trump the latter and take the trick. We saw in discussing Maklay's promise (Chapter 3) the kind of example that may be in mind.

This belief in the general overridingness of Millian 'moral' considerations does not, however, seem to me defensible, and one may wonder why it is held. That it is may have something to do with the special position of certain prohibitions that as a matter of fact all have to do with what Mill counted as morality. For a good case can be made out for a limited moral absolutism by which certain such actions are held to be such as to rule out circumstances in which it could ever be right to perform them. Adultery and lying have been suggested as having this character, though I myself would not agree with Aristotle, Aquinas, or Anscombe about either. I think especially ludicrous to suggest, for instance, that those fighting with the

[20] P. F. Naish, Chairman, Prevention of Heart Attacks and Strokes Enterprise, North Staffordshire Royal Infirmary: letter in the *Independent*, 17 Aug. 1991 (italics mine).

Resistance against the Nazis should not if necessary have lied through their teeth to protect themselves or their comrades. An absolute moral ban on torture seems, however, to be another matter. If the frequently unchallengeable description 'torture' applies to an action, then, whatever the circumstances, it is in my firm opinion morally 'out'.[21] But 'moral absolutism' of this ilk does not support any general theory of the overridingness of those reasons for action that could be called 'moral reasons' in Mill's lexicon. Nor is it pertinent here to recall a number of descriptions of action that are what I should like to call 'conceptually verdictive' from a practical point of view, in that they entail a 'final' 'should' or 'should not'. 'Unjust' is, for instance, such a description, as is 'cruel'. If and when it is unjust or cruel to withhold from someone something one owes that person, then one necessarily acts badly in doing so. It may be hard to know whether in a particular case withholding the money really is cruel or unjust: perhaps a debtor's children will go hungry if he discharges the debt—a dilemma that must only too often face a borrower in the Third World. But one who decides that the debt must in justice or charity be paid cannot, at the same time, deny that he will be acting wrongly if he does not pay it. Perhaps it will be thought that all such verdictives give judgement in favour of a consideration that has to do with the rights or needs of others, or with public morality. But this, even if so, would be of little consequence; and in any case it is not so, as we see if we consider words such as 'imprudent' or 'foolish'. For these too are verdictive, contrasting in this respect with expressions such as 'dangerous' and 'self-regarding'. The latter descriptions can be applied to an action without implying that it should not be done, whereas this is not true of words such as 'imprudent' and 'foolish'.

Nor is it difficult to find examples where, in a clash of reasons for and against an action, it is not the 'other-related' consideration that should have the final vote. There are of course many situations in

---

[21] I was glad to see an article by Ronald Dworkin that supports this opinion ('Report from Hell', *New York Review of Books*, 17 July 1986). He sees the ban on torture as a barrier to the power of a tyrannical ruler. One might also see torture as the ultimate negation of the impulse humans have to come to each other's aid.

which one obligation overrides another; but as Bernard Williams has memorably put it, not all overridings of presumptive moral obligations work on the principle 'Obligation out—obligation in'.[22] To see this we have only to go back to our example of the person in bed with flu. Suppose this patient had promised to go to help a friend on the day on which he is ill. Unless the promise were a very solemn promise, or the breaking of it very serious for the promisee, he will be able to say in exoneration, 'I am sorry, but I was not able to get out that day.' It is not that his legs would have failed him, but rather that there was something else that he should, all things considered, have done, that is, to keep to his bed. In fact it is often reasonable for agents to give themselves (never mind their families) preference over others. As John Taurek pointed out some time ago in an excellent article, it is not at all generally believed that, for example, one should incur the certainty of losing a limb even to save another from injury more serious than that.[23] The slogan 'Moral considerations are overriding considerations' expresses not a truth of moral philosophy but an implausible doctrine about what should be done.

My opponent in the main line of our controversy may protest that my attention to a wide class of evaluations has, in taking us outside the realm of obligation and duty, also taken us outside moral philosophy. One might say, 'So much the worse for moral philosophy!' I do not, as I have said, much care how the word 'moral' is used. But it seems important to recognize as virtues of the will (as volitional excellences) a readiness to accept good things for oneself, and to see the great importance for life of the self-regarding aspect of virtues such as hope and a readiness to accept good things.[24] And on the negative side, we might want to use the description 'moral fault' in thinking of the kind of timidity, conventionality, and wilful self-abnegation that may spoil no one's life but one's own. That we tend to speak in moral philosophy only of volitional faults that impinge particularly on others gives the whole subject an objectionably rigoristic, prissy, moralistic tone that we would hardly care to take up

[22] Williams, *Ethics and the Limits of Philosophy*, 180.

[23] Taurek, 'Should the Numbers Count?'.

[24] A graduate student once said that my lectures had first made him see 'that to be anti-sex could be immoral'. I liked that.

in everyday life. It also tends to cloud understanding by suggesting that there is a special meaning for words such as 'ought' in such contexts. In fact 'ought' is very close to 'should', and if we speak of 'a moral context' this usually simply indicates the presence of a reason for acting that has to do with others rather than oneself.

6

Happiness and Human Good

I have argued earlier that it is wrong to look for an independent criterion of practical rationality to which goodness in action must somehow be shown to conform. Instead, rational choice should be seen as an aspect of human goodness, standing at the heart of the virtues rather than out there on its own.

I now want to discuss in more detail an objection to my view of practical rationality: an objection that stands in a threatening posture just offstage. I mean the thought that practical rationality is the pursuit, and nothing but the pursuit, of happiness. Nothing was said in the last chapter about happiness. Surely that was rather odd, considering the importance of the topic in the history of moral philosophy? How can rationality of action be discussed without a word about the relation between virtue and happiness? Is not happiness humanity's good?

I must now try to place the concept of happiness within the foregoing account of the goodness of human action. If vice is 'a form of natural defect' and virtue goodness of the will, where in the schema of natural normativity does the idea of human happiness belong?

I want to tackle this problem head-on. But first it should be separated from the once influential, now largely discredited, idea that no one ever *does* (can) pursue anything except his or her own happiness. This was a theory based on a heady mixture of conceptual intuition and psychological scepticism: the first probably coming from a confused acknowledgement of real conceptual relations between the concepts of desire, achievement, and satisfaction; the second from the everyday observation that people often seek their own happiness while denying that they do. Neither psychological hedonism nor psychological egoism can be established in either way. Happiness is not the universal aim of action. Brave people choose great and immediate evils, such as certain death, in order to rescue or defend others. And even in their choice of lives some reject happiness for the sake of some other goal.[1]

What is problematic for morality about the relation between virtue and happiness does not come from the direction of such theories as psychological hedonism or psychological egoism, but rather from the idea that happiness is Man's good, together with the thought that *happiness may be successfully pursued through evil action.* For then it would seem that there is an independent criterion of rational action—the pursuit of happiness—with rationality on occasion demanding what virtue forbids.

Indeed, the thought that happiness is humanity's good may seem to disrupt the argument of the preceding chapters on natural normativity through the idea that the instantiation of the human life form lies in happiness, which should therefore be the determinant of virtue. For how then could it be that virtue sometimes requires the sacrifice of happiness? And how is it that happiness can, it seems, be obtained by wickedness? Can these things be denied?

In the following pages I shall do my best to sort out this tangled skein of ideas, though recognizing that my best efforts are going to be pretty pathetic in this deep and difficult part of moral philosophy. Later in this chapter I shall question the assumption that happiness can be taken *tout court* to be Man's good, arguing that on some interpretations of the word 'happiness' this is unacceptable. Firstly, however, full justice must be done to the thought that happiness can successfully be pursued through doing evil. I shall therefore give a sketch of happiness as there construed, with the plea that we should not *too quickly* reject each and every picture of wickedness and happiness conjoined.

It may be useful, however, to begin even further back than this,

---

[1] When told that marriage to Nijinsky would ruin her life, the future Madame Nijinska replied, 'I am going to marry him in spite of everything . . . I'd rather be unhappy serving Nijinsky's genius than be happy without him.' Romola Nijinsky, *Nijinsky*, 204.

by saying something about the different ways in which happiness is predicated of human beings—as we speak, for example, of their being happy doing something, being in a happy frame of mind, or having a happy life. Some of these different predications will make their separate appearances in this discussion of the relation of happiness to virtue; so one needs to have a variety of uses in mind.

Let us begin with the proposition that someone is happy doing something or other. What is intended here may be quite minimal: when we say 'happy φ-ing' we may signify nothing more than an absence of restlessness, or efforts to change a situation, so that we can say even of an animal that, for instance, it is 'quite happy where it is'. And when said of human beings, who, unlike animals, can be contented or discontented, 'happy doing such and such' may simply connote an absence of discontent. 'Happy φ-ing' is, however, more likely to tell of enjoyment, or pleasure, or liking-to-do: here enjoyment comes on the scene, as something that must, one would think, be part of a happy *life*.

Enjoyment is a difficult concept. Activities are most often what people are said to enjoy, and when they enjoy such things as holidays or jobs, enjoying activities will be a large part of what is meant. It does, however, make sense, though it is rare, to speak of enjoying the fact that such and such; and it turns out, interestingly enough, that enjoyment of activities often involves thoughts. For although one can enjoy sex, or eating and drinking, or movement, simply on account of what it is pleasurable to feel, it would be hard to explain enjoyment of philosophy, or even of gardening, in these terms. In a whole range of such cases, what seems to be important to the enjoyment is the perception of something seen as good. Often achievement itself will be the good, and that may be all there is to it, as *What* when someone is doing a crossword puzzle or some other thing that *results* in itself is pointless. But it may also be *what* is being achieved that is *in bad* seen as good in itself. So if there were a people who accompanied *× good?* their activities with variable movements of a hand, and a steady hum, we might find ourselves translating the first as, roughly, 'Good, I'm getting on', and the second as, 'Good, something desirable is being achieved', when each could, in the absence of negative factors, be seen as an expression of enjoyment. What is remarkable is that both of these bits of language would be propositional. I have been struck by how much the enjoyment of gardening is like this. It owes, I find, little to pleasant sensation or movement and much to awareness both of immediate achievement ('That's got it well dug in!') and the prospect of good things to come; so that goodness is here prior to enjoyment, as well as (in some sense) implied by it; and the same is no doubt true of enjoying doing philosophy. What we have here is propositional, though not, of course, such as to require episodes of thought, because it is a sense of how things are, and therefore not essentially episodic. It may seem puzzlingly like a coloured film over the surface of the mind until it is noticed that it has the distinctive relation to the time sequence that belongs to a belief. Beliefs, which even if long-standing may never have been formulated by the one who has them, can be attributed to him or her in the present tense, irrespective of whether, at the time of attribution, they occupy the mind.[2]

This is one way in which thoughts, and particularly the thought of good, plays a part in happiness, but it is not the only way. For so far we have been dealing only with enjoyment, and enjoyment does not have to be seen as the chief element in happiness. If someone has much to enjoy in his life this is at least a factor counting in favour of his happiness. But happiness is also a matter of that to which one might give the general title of gladness. Sometimes the gladness will attach to particular moments, as when good news is heard, or good things especially salient in one's mind, but gladness, unlike enjoyment, does not as such occupy clockable time, and this part of happiness too may take the form of a *sense* of things being well, rather than of thoughts that occupy the mind. Being contented, by and large, with the way things are in one's life, or at least being conscious of the good things in it, is obviously a large part of happiness, and the question 'Are you happy?' may ask someone how it is with him or her precisely in this respect.

Finally, in this brief sketch of some of the different contexts in

---

[2] Wittgenstein stressed the importance of differences in the way that different 'psychological concepts' were 'clockable'. See *Remarks on the Philosophy of Psychology*, vol. ii, sections 43–63.

which the term 'happy' and its cognates are found, we should note the expression 'a happy frame of mind', which describes a mood in which someone is cheerful, confident, ready for enjoyment, and apt to have a sense of things being well. That things are well with him may be what he really believes, but a happy mood is something so much on the surface that it can cover up actual knowledge that things are not well at all.

It is evident, however, that what has been said so far is quite inadequate as an account of that sense of the word in which it can be said that happiness is humanity's good. For one recalls Wittgenstein's famous death-bed insistence that he had had a wonderful life, which I have never seen questioned as the truth. Interpreted in terms of happy states of mind it would, however, have been very puzzling indeed if a life as troubled as his had been described as a good life. What Wittgenstein said rang true because of the things he had done, with rare passion and genius, and especially on account of his philosophy. Did he not say elsewhere 'The joy of my thoughts is the joy of my own strange life'?[3] Joy is of the essence of a good life, but is of course compatible with prolonged suffering. In this connection I think also of an old Quaker woman of whom I have read, who after much persecution and suffering spoke of her 'joyous life' preaching the Word. She did not speak of her life as a happy life; it would have been puzzling if she had. So this example, too, helps us to question the identity of meaning between the expressions 'a good life' and 'a happy life' if the latter is thought of simply in terms of contentment, enjoyment, or pleasure.

Contentment is not only not necessary but also not sufficient for a happiness that could convincingly be called humanity's good. I recall a talk by a doctor who described a patient of his (who had perhaps had a prefrontal lobotomy) as 'perfectly happy all day long picking up leaves'. This impressed me because I thought, 'Well, most of us are not happy all day long doing the things we do', and realized how strange it would be to think that the very kindest of fathers would arrange such an operation for his (perfectly normal) child.

---

[3] 'Die Freude an meinem Gedanken ist die Freude an meinem eigenen seltsamen Leben.' MS of 1931, quoted by Norman Malcolm, *Ludwig Wittgenstein: A Memoir*, 84.

Such a procedure would of course be dangerous, because who knows in an uncertain world whether the servants paid to provide leaves or simple toys for the whole of the child's life would really do that? Setting this aside, we can suppose ourselves looking back in the life of a man or woman who has in fact spent a lifetime in child-ish pursuits. That he or she was perfectly happy doing this is a description that could really apply. But the example shows that when we talk about a happiness that is supposed to be humanity's good we cannot intend pleasure or contentment alone. As Aristotle remarked, we should not wish to continue in the pleasures of child-hood at the cost of remaining a child.[4]

What, then, is the elusive concept of *happiness* that could rightly be given a central role in moral philosophy? Most people would say that it is a state of mind, and there is no doubt something correct about that. Nevertheless the mistake may lie right here. For the description inclines us to think of the concept of *happiness* as if it had the same logical grammar as that of, for example, *excitement* or *ela-tion*, and that is not right. To see this we may return to the idea of a child's pleasure, asking why Aristotle was right to dismiss the thought that we would exchange this for the things that can be good in an adult life. What is it that is *in its nature* impossible for a child? It is not intense pleasure—a child can have that. Nor is it a state of mind such as excitement or elation that can be predicated wherever there are certain signs: squealing and giggling, for instance, and beg-ging for more of whatever it is that pleases the child so much. And we can of course say of a child that he or she 'is happy' paddling or building sandcastles. What seems to be missing—and necessarily missing—is the dimension of depth: a dimension that we cannot count as irrelevant to the happiness-as-good of a grown-up. We are mistaken if we think of happiness as something 'in the mind' in principle detachable from a person's resources of experience and belief, as if a mental state were like the surface of a pond that could be described in terms of the coming and going of water beetles there, without any reference to what was lower down.

The important point is that such an idea of deep happiness is

---

[4] Aristotle, *Nicomachean Ethics*, Book X, chapter 3, 1174a1–3.

completely wrong, and I think further enquiry will be useful in spite of the fact that the idea of *depth* in human feeling and thought is itself not easy to explain.[5] We should remind ourselves that the use of the word 'deep' as applied, for example, to love, to friendship, or to happiness is something that we have been able to learn like any other part of language, and therefore has public criteria. Yet the difficulties are real. For the thoughts that may afflict one here are exceedingly odd. I have caught myself in the ridiculous thought that what is deep must have something to do with taking a deep breath, or with what is deep within one's carapace like one's viscera or one's heart. A slightly more sensible but still quite mistaken suggestion is that the deep is what causes a lot of disturbance in our lives. That cannot be right, because we understand someone very well if he says on his death-bed that he wasted his life on trivial things; and things that do not really matter—like a bad *faux pas*, or the non-arrival of an invitation to a party of the duchesse de Guermantes—can create any amount of disturbance, right up to obsession. It is no good saying that they do not bring *deep* feelings, since the concept of depth is just what we are trying to understand. Nor will it do to think that whatever someone minds about on his death-bed is what he feels deeply about, since all sorts of strange things may be said there.[6]

What is characteristic of each of these suggestions is that it is reductive: one is trying to find some less puzzling *substitute* for the troublesome proposition about what is deep. But perhaps this is itself a mistake. Perhaps 'deep', as used in the way in which we are interested, yields what we might call a 'ground-floor' expression and so, though it has some traceable connections with what is not physically on the surface of things, has surroundings of its own that

[5] I once discussed the difficult concept of depth in life and literature with Isaiah Berlin. Years later I asked him whether the problem still worried him, to which he replied in his much imitated but inimitable voice, 'I think about it *all* the time, *all* the time.' Whether he would have agreed with what I have said here I have sadly no way of knowing, but he emphatically rejected the 'disturbance' theory which I go on to discuss.

[6] William Pitt the Younger's last words may have been 'Oh my country, how I leave my country!', but in a different report, 'I think I could eat one of Bellamy's veal pies.' See Lord Rosebery, *Pitt*, 269 and Appendix D.

partly determine its meaning in a psychological context.[7] One can
say that bona fide attributions of deep happiness take place in a
characteristic syndrome of spontaneous utterance, action, gesture,
and response. But what is at least as important to the discussion of
the connection between virtue and happiness is that there is also a
restriction of cause and object. This is shown by the fact that it does
not make sense, without a very special background, to suggest that
someone found deep happiness, in, say, a running victory in a dispute with a neighbour over a morning newspaper or a milk bottle,
however much we think of 'fizzy' behaviour and elation. Whereas
deep happiness and joy over the birth of a child? That is a different
matter![8] It is not just what someone says but what he says it *about*
that matters, and why should it not be so? We are tempted to think
of deep happiness as explicable psychologically *in a way that makes it
possible to separate it from its objects.* But why should this be possible?
Why shouldn't the communality of meaning not depend here on a
shared reaction among human beings to certain things that are very
general in human life? Are not these reactions shared even by people of very different cultures; not, of course, exactly, but nevertheless with sufficient similarity for people of one age or culture to
understand depth of happiness over a birth and depth of grief about
the death of parent, child, or friend?

Thus possible objects of deep happiness seem to be things that are
basic in human life, such as home, and family, and work, and friendship. They are, in a way, ordinary things, even though, in a person
such as Wittgenstein, the chief joy of his life was in the quest for
truth, and in other exceptional men and women it is in artistic cre-
ation or the exploration of strange lands. Most people, of course,
find their greatest happiness in more mundane surroundings. I
think, as illustration, of a story of Gertrude Stein's in which she
writes of a rather simple woman, Anna, who was in service with a

[handwritten margin note: universal goods?]

---

[7] It is relevant here to remember Wittgenstein's insistence that what is in the language has 'need of public criteria'. See, e.g., *Philosophical Investigations*, section 580.

[8] An American statesman, Grover Cleveland, who had already held the highest
office in the land, wrote to a friend after the birth of a longed-for child, 'Today I took
my first steps in the real world.'

doctor and cooked for him and his bachelor friends. Stein says that this was a very happy time in Anna's life.[9] The description 'deep happiness' seems in order here. Why? Well, they ate so much, and Anna had a good job to do and a proud place in the world.

Similarly, there is the case of Caleb Garth in George Eliot's *Middlemarch*, a character who is a bit solemn for our taste, but definitely the salt of the earth. In the passage that interests me he is reporting to his wife the news that he has been asked to manage part of Sir James Cheetam's country estate:

It's a fine bit of work, Susan! A man without a family would be glad to do it for nothing . . . [I]t's a fine thing to come to a man when he's seen into the nature of business: to have the chance of getting a bit of the country into good fettle as they say. . . . I'd sooner have it than a fortune. I hold it the most honourable work that is.[10]

Once again, it seems to me, we have an indication of deep happiness, understandable particularly if we remember the predominance of agriculture in the economy of England at the time of which George Eliot wrote. To get a bit of land into good shape was to do something important, having to do with getting food; also with improving the tenants' houses, which was a particular concern of Garth's. Land was home and livelihood to oneself and others, and it would have been with a sense of such things in the background that he expressed a special kind of pleasure at being given the job.

I want to draw from these examples, and in general from the discussion of deep happiness, the thought that we should be suspicious of the idea that whenever we speak of happiness we are speaking of a state of mind which seems as detachable from beliefs about special objects as is, for example, having a headache, or a tune running though one's head.[11] It seems to me that this picture should be shaken by a realization of the impossibility of attributing a grown-up's deep happiness to a young child. If we say that 'that' might happen to be found 'there', we must surely ask 'But what, now, is *that*?'

[9] Stein, 'The Good Anna', 33.

[10] Eliot, *Middlemarch*, 431.

[11] Not that even these are really states of mind, though philosophers often speak of them as such, and perhaps fall into confusion on that account.

It seems certain, therefore, that we must go beyond the description of a life of pleasure and contentment in looking into the concept of human happiness. It is not enough, however, to say that a life of trivial pleasures and contentment cannot plausibly be identified with a life that is good in the sense that Wittgenstein must have intended when he spoke of having had a wonderful life. Something important is still missing, because, though it seems that this must be problematic, we have not yet said anything decisive against the conjunction of even the greatest, deepest, happiness with wickedness.

This new problem is one that has for me centred round an example that I constructed on reading long ago of a Nazi who had had a leading role in the running of one of Hitler's death camps and was reported as saying in later years that 'whatever happened next' he would not be 'the real loser'. He had, he said, thoroughly enjoyed living in Brazil and had not thought much about the past. As I discovered only recently, this particular man—Gustav Wagner—was deceiving himself: he became suicidal later on. Perhaps there is always a price to pay for wickedness, in real self-esteem or in the possibilities of loving relations with others.[12]

I am, however, dissatisfied with such a solution to this new problem. It puts too much weight on a rather uncertain hypothesis. What do I really know about the possibility of combining wickedness and happiness? Drawing on the literature about men of his ilk, can we not realistically suppose that a certain Nazi commandant—call him 'Z'—enjoyed his 'work' in the camp as he made the day-to-day arrangements for the death of great numbers of men, women, and children in the gas chambers? Going about his tasks in good spirits, in a happy frame of mind, he could have had a sense of achievement in solving administrative problems; on occasions he might himself have selected prisoners for death or for 'punishment', taking pleasure in his power to terrify them and to have them destroyed or spared at the wave of a hand.

Nor can we avoid our dilemma by reminding ourselves that hap-

---

[12] How could Hitler and others around him have had anything more than a sentimental love of children when they were ready to have even one single child driven into a gas chamber?

piness is not just a matter of enjoyment, cheerful mood, and happy occupation, but must extend all the way into the underlying thoughts that a person has about himself and his life. For here, too, 'Z' may seem to score. He was not ashamed of the pleasure he took in tormenting and destroying the inmates of the camp; on the contrary, he thought that he was helping to purify the Aryan race, inspired by Hitler's leadership and serving a great cause. If we say that he could not really have been contented we are trying to get the facts to conform to a picture of the way we think they *must* be. This in itself should suggest that something philosophically interesting is in the offing. For Wittgenstein has told us to focus attention on just such inclinations to say 'must', and has taught us to expect to find in them not truth but rather the crooked reflection of a real 'grammatical' (meaning conceptual) truth.[13]

In the following pages I shall try not to forget what the facts do really allow us to believe about the ordinary human goods of affection and friendship that are necessarily forfeited by one who, like our 'Z', has a profound lack of humanity. But I want to explore the thought that a tendency to go beyond what we really observe reflects a conceptual truth that is still to be exposed. To be sure, we have already dismissed mere contentment as identical with human good, arguing that the dimension of depth in happiness must be taken into account, and querying the claim of the wicked to have had lives that are as happy as can be. Yet there is surely something fundamental about the relation between human virtue and human good that is missing still.

To get even an inkling of what this might be it is necessary, I think, to go right back to the conceptual connection that is at the core of the idea of natural goodness as understood in this book.

Let us think once more about plants and animals and ask about the relationship between goodness and defect in an individual and what counts as flourishing for a member of the species to which it belongs. To flourish is here to instantiate the life form of that species, and to know whether an individual is or is not as it should be, one must know the life form of the species. A quite general conceptual

[13] See Wittgenstein, *Philosophical Investigations*, section 66.

connection between life form and goodness is given specification in the myriad life forms of different kinds of living things; no doubt historically by an evolutionary story that leaves the members of each species dependent not only on their own internal resources but also on the environment to which the species came to be adapted.

Given that goodness in respect of bodily health, of faculties such as intelligence and memory, and so on is precisely that which fits a living thing for the instantiation of the life form of its species, and that this counts as the good of a living thing, then in so far as this instantiation in humans can be identified with having a good life, the question that concerns us in this chapter is the relation between virtue and a good life and the connection of that with the happiness of the one whose life it is. So far, as for instance in considering the case of 'Z', we have supposed that conceptually speaking we must allow that a wicked character could have an extremely happy life. But I now want to argue that we find in our own thought a way of understanding human good and even human happiness that does not allow of such a combination. It may be suggested that such usages are merely pious, depending on a religious faith that defines true happiness in religious terms, as perhaps the contemplation of the Deity, or a happiness to be thought in terms of a Muslim afterlife. I think, however, that this would be a mistake, and that there is something here to be recognized by people of all faiths or none. This is, however, an extremely difficult subject. It is too quick to say that because human *goodness* belongs to those who have the virtues, human *good* is what they will attain in acting well.[14]

What, we may ask, are we even talking about if we speak of human good? And given the fantastic diversity of human lives can we really think of a *species-wide* notion of human good at all? Is it even clear what terms we should use at this point? We can speak of a human being as flourishing, but as applied to members of the

---

[14] Neither Elizabeth Anscombe nor Gavin Lawrence is a philosopher to be accused of hastiness in thought. But I wish they would not move from accounts of the merely clever practical inferences of the one whose ends are bad straight to the assertion that he 'gets a great evil for himself'. To be sure, Aristotle seems to say just this when discussing practical inference in the *Nicomachean Ethics*, Book VI, chapter 9, 1142b17–20. But the question is, what should lead us to accept what he says?

ᴎan race this has too special a connotation, in that it suggests
ʰoubled success. We accepted Wittgenstein's description of his
ᴀs a good life, but to give so troubled a man as an example of one
ᴑ had flourished would suggest a special philosophical use of the
ns.

ᴵndeed, there may be an unwelcome whiff of philosophy even in
ᴀking of human good. One is tempted to use capitals, as if we
re quite at home with the idea, for instance in the question 'Is
happiness Man's Good?', and in speaking like this we may already
lose ourselves. There is nothing wrong with giving a word or an
expression a special meaning in philosophy, but then its meaning
must really be made clear. Otherwise an obtruding picture may lead
us to invent a logical grammar in a way that will likely foul up the
debate.[15]

How then shall we avoid such rarefactions in thinking about
human good, while yet avoiding the too special implications of a
word such as 'flourishing'? I think that we may get a first glimpse of
our quarry by considering the concept of *benefit* as this is applicable
in the domain of life. Let us ask what it is to benefit a living thing, as
this seems, after all, to be the same as doing something that is for its
good. The concept of benefit seems to have the right kind of gener-
ality, and will of course cover both a beneficial change in an organism and that which protects it from external harm. To benefit an
individual it may be necessary to act on it—to make it better—or on
the other hand to act on its environment. St Jerome healed the
lion's paw but Noah sheltered his animals from the flood.[16] We may
notice in passing, however, that neither making a plant, animal,
or person better by providing what makes him or it better, like

[15] I think, for instance of the way philosophers tend to speak of 'the mind' while
pointing at their heads. No one points at his head when saying 'I haven't made up my
mind' or 'My mind is all confused', and a teacher has no special reason to think of a
student's head while describing the qualities of his mind.

[16] I would add at this point that animals cannot be said to be flourishing if they are
not living anything like a natural life. An animal is not benefited by being kept alive by
artificial feeding and induced to breed by artificial means, because such a life would be
too far from its life form. What fitted such an unnaturally fixed-up animal for survival,
such as extreme docility, might not be goodness but perhaps defect in a thing of its
kind.

medicine, nor improving environmental circumstances, is necessarily beneficial as things work out. St Jerome would not have benefited the lion had it leaped forward in relief from pain, but fallen straight into a trap. And going back to humans, we notice that there have been times when it was precisely the healthy men who were sent to the mines, and that humane doctors working in the hospitals (the 'sick barracks') of Hitler's or Stalin's death-dealing labour camps were sometimes careful that their patients should not get back to work too fast.

Let us now consider the concept of benefit specifically in relation to human beings, using the discussion as a first step to an understanding of the idea of happiness that would disallow the combination of wickedness and felicity in the case of our fictional but only too lifelike 'Z'. To begin the discussion, I would here call on a common understanding of the idea of benefit. For suppose that we think of some really wicked persons such as the serial killers Frederick and Rosemary West, who did not even spare their own children in their career of abuse and murder. For many years they were able to act out their sexual fantasies free from detection, and might well have continued to do so to the end of their natural lives. What then would it have been right to say about the contribution of those whose behaviour made this kind of thing possible? Would they have *benefited* the horrible Wests? It seems to me that in our natural refusal to say so we glimpse a conceptual truth that does not usually lie so clearly on the surface. And that if the usual conceptual connections hold here, as they surely do, between benefit and what is for someone's good, what has come to the surface is also about that.

That happiness can be seen in this way—as conceptually inseparable from virtue—is shown, I believe, more closely in another example that has puzzled me for many years. I am thinking of the case of some very brave men who opposed the Nazis.[17] I know about most of these particular people, many of whom were very young, from letters published in a book called *Dying We Live*, which should

---

[17] Many discussions with Gavin Lawrence have kept this case continually in my mind and helped me very much.

be better known than it is.[18] These are letters from prisoners about to be executed after trial in Nazi Germany: letters written to their wives, or parents, or sweethearts, which, because of that, give a very poignant sense of what it was that they were losing in laying down their lives. At the time when the letters were written, the die was already cast: probably no one of them could have escaped death whatever he might have said or done. But earlier, as when, for instance, a pastor among them had refused to stop preaching against the ill-treatment of Jewish people, they must have had a choice between the life they could have had with their families, and the death that awaited them in prison. In any case no one of them would, I am sure, have been willing to try to buy better treatment at the end by renouncing his anti-Nazi allegiance. So let us adapt the example and suppose that when they wrote the letters they still had such a choice.

I think that, as so developed, this is a particularly interesting case because, as already suggested, but for the dreadful times they lived in most of these men—let us call them the Letter-Writers—might have had especially happy lives. The letters give the impression that those who wrote them were especially well fitted for the enjoyment of the best things in life: for great happiness. So one may very naturally say that they knowingly sacrificed their happiness in making their choice. And yet this does not seem to be the only thing we could say. One may think that there was a sense in which the Letter-Writers did, *but also a sense in which they did not*, sacrifice their happiness in refusing to go along with the Nazis. In the abstract what they so longed for—to get back to their families—was of course wholly good. But as they were placed it was impossible to pursue this end by just and honourable means. And this, I suggest, explains the sense in which they did not see as their happiness what they could have got by giving in. Happiness in life, they might have said, was not something possible for them.[19] It may seem that one can get to

[18] H. Gollwitzer, K. Kuhn, and R. Schneider (eds.), *Dying We Live: The Final Messages and Records of Some Germans who Defied Hitler.*

[19] Readers of these letters have been struck by the extraordinary sense of happiness that they radiate, which has perhaps to do with the fact that practically all the writers

the bottom of this matter simply by thinking about the shame that men of the Letter-Writers' calibre would no doubt have felt, in later life, had they gone along with the Nazis. This is of course important, for they might have felt that everything that came later was corroded by the fact that it had been gained by acting in this way. Yet this is not the heart of the matter. For supposing that they had been offered a 'Lethe-drug' that would have taken from them all future knowledge of the action? They would not have accepted. And there would have been a way in which *they would not have felt that happiness lay in acceptance*.[20] It is the latter difficult thought that I want to hold on to, and to understand. At the very least its presence gives us a clear indication that happiness isolated from virtue is not the only way in which the concept is to be found in our thoughts.

The suggestion is, then, that humanity's good can be thought of as happiness, and yet in such a way that combining it with wickedness is a priori ruled out. Wittgenstein in speaking of his life as a wonderful life certainly did not mean that it had been a life of virtue; but I am sure that he would not have counted as a source of happiness anything he saw as evil in it. Of course, if perfection were in question no human life could be a good life and the concept would have no application. Nevertheless, when Aristotle gave an introductory account of *eudaimonia* in terms of activity in accordance with virtue, in Book I of the *Nicomachean Ethics*, he described something of which we too have, it seems, an idea. He insisted that the life of one who could be counted as *eudaimon* required

were devout Christians who thought of themselves as carrying out a task laid on them by God. One recognizes that such beliefs must often fail to sustain someone in terrible circumstances. Yet even there a brave man or woman might *under a certain description* be glad of what had happened; as someone thrown back unconscious into his cell after torture might say 'Good!' on realizing that he had not given information; in spite of a consuming dread of what would happen next day.

[20] To see it as happiness they would have to have changed, and would not have accepted the prospect of such a change. The case is not like that of, say, a retiring person who cannot imagine himself happy in a public role, but might nevertheless be glad if he could change himself. Related to this is the fact that one would not wish for the sake of someone one loved that 'in the tight corner' they would be able to forsake their virtue in time; which shows the inadequacy of a 'virtue ethic' theory that makes much of the fact that *they would not be able* all at once to change a deep-seated disposition to act in a certain way.

favourable external circumstances. No one, he said, could so describe Priam given the great misfortunes he suffered in the sacking of his city and the loss of his sons. Yet operation according to virtue, whatever the virtues might later be shown to be, was the essence of the concept of *eudaimonia* itself as introduced in Book I of the *Nicomachean Ethics*.

The conclusion of the present chapter is that *happiness* is a protean concept, appearing now in one way and now in another. There was nothing wrong with what the doctor said of his patient who was 'perfectly happy all day picking up leaves'. And there is also a sad truth to be recognized in the saying about the wicked who flourish like the bay tree. But there is a third interpretation of the word happiness: the one in which we must understand someone who in sacrificing his life for the sake of justice would not have said that he was sacrificing his happiness, but rather that a happy life had turned out not to be possible for him. We cannot ignore this interpretation of the concept if we identify happiness with human good.

In terms of contemporary discussions of happiness and its relation to virtue, I should describe my own view in the following terms. I agree with John McDowell that we have an understanding of the word 'happiness' that is close to Aristotle's *eudaimonia* in that operation in conformity with the virtues belongs to its meaning.[21] In my own terminology 'happiness' is here understood as *the enjoyment of good things*, meaning enjoyment in attaining, and in pursuing, right ends. I do not, however, accept McDowell's apparent *identification* of happiness with a life of virtue, or his idea that a loss incurred through an action necessary for virtue is 'no loss at all'. He seems to me to allow too little for the genuine tragedy that there may be in a moral choice. I myself would rather say that there is indeed a kind of happiness that only goodness can achieve, but that by one of the evil chances of life it may be out of the reach of even the best of men.

I believe that in thus disagreeing with McDowell I am agreeing with what David Wiggins has said against what he calls McDowell's 'rigorism'. I should also like to draw attention to Wiggins's excellent

---

[21] See especially McDowell, 'The Role of *Eudaimonia* in Aristotle's Ethics' and 'Eudaimonism and Realism in Aristotle's Ethics'.

desire to bring Hume's theory of the human sentiments into the debate at this point. For there is a way in which a good person must not only see his or her good as bound up with goodness of desire and action, but also *feel* that it is, with sentiments such as pleasure, pride, and honour.[22]

---

[22] See Wiggins, 'Eudaimonism and Realism in Aristotle's Ethics: A Reply to John McDowell'.

7

Immoralism

Immoralism is nowadays a somewhat neglected subject: one can search the indexes of dozens of contemporary works without finding a single entry under this heading. Many contemporary moral philosophers seem to agree with Prichard who, notoriously, scolded Plato for accepting the challenge of immoralists such as Thrasymachus and Callicles (in the *Republic* and the *Gorgias*) to show that the just man was happier than the unjust.[1] And while Nietzsche's work now interests many analytic philosophers, one finds few who actually try to confront him. This seems to me a mistake, if only because the whole idea of immoralism is hard to understand. Nietzsche said that he was attacking the premises of morality. Does it then have premises? What could these be? I want to consider the subject of immoralism in the light of the account of moral evaluation given in previous chapters of the present book.

In the *Republic* the immoralist case is put forward by the Sophist Thrasymachus and (as Devil's advocates) by the brothers Glaucon and Adeimantus who are not satisfied with Socrates' way of refuting Thrasymachus in Book I.[2] Thrasymachus had said that justice (that is, the just actions of just men) served the interests of the stronger, identifying the stronger first as the rulers who lay down laws to their own advantage, but later as strong, ruthless individuals who swindle honest men in such matters as contracts, 'plundering by fraud and force alike the goods of others, sacred and holy things, private and public possessions, and never pettily but always on a grand scale'.[3]

---

[1] H. A. Prichard, 'Duty and Interest'.
[2] Plato, *Republic*, Books I–II, 336B–367E.   [3] Ibid. 344A.

These strong men, powerful enough to escape retribution, profited
from the self-inflicted injury of the just, whose obedience was not
virtue but silly good nature. Therefore the life of the unjust was
superior to that of the just. The strong who practised injustice followed good policy (*euboulia*) and were wise and good (*phronimoi* and
agathoi). So it was wrong to prize justice over injustice.

Socrates tied Thrasymachus up in knots, but left Glaucon and
Adeimantus dissatisfied: they thought that Socrates had failed to
refute the strongest arguments in favour of injustice, and were
ready to put them forward on the Sophist's behalf. They wanted to
be confirmed in their view that the life of the just is better than that
of the unjust. Glaucon therefore argues, in the role of an immoralist,
that most people think injustice *in itself* better than justice, praising
the latter only for the rewards that society attaches to it. It is true
that justice is better for those who cannot get away with injustice,
but the life of the strong unjust man is best of all. Those who praise
and practise justice do so only because they fear injustice: unable to
live the best of lives, they settle for the second best, which is neither
to suffer nor to do injustice. They practise justice unwillingly and
from inability to inflict injustice, as is proved by the fact that no one
of them would act justly if, through a magic ring of invisibility, they
could become invulnerable. If someone with such a power refrained
from plunder he would not be admired but rather seen as the most
foolish of men.

Glaucon asks Socrates to show that justice is better than injustice
in itself as existing in the soul, quite apart from penalties and
rewards, and suggests that in the argument they should strip these
away, contrasting the life of a just man reputed unjust with one
unjust but reputed just. Glaucon himself believes that justice is one
of those good things desired for what they are in themselves as well
as for their consequences. He wants Socrates to show that this is so,
thus comparing justice to thought, sight, and health, rather than to
gymnastic exercises or medical treatment which, though advanta-
geous in their outcome, are troublesome in themselves. Adeimantus
too presses this request, asking Socrates to show that injustice is the
greatest of evils in the soul of him who has it, and justice the greatest good. Otherwise, he says, the best policy will be to be unjust and

not be found out. It will not be justice but the appearance of justice that men should seek.

These then are the elements in the immoralist position as represented in Books I and II of the *Republic*. Socrates assailed it by accepting the request of Glaucon and Adeimantus to show what justice is in the soul: that it is health rather than disorder there. He denied that happiness lies in the possession of wealth and power or any other of the advantages listed by Thrasymachus, insisting that it rather lay in harmony in the soul.

It is not relevant to the thesis of the present book that I should consider the arguments developed in the remainder of the *Republic*. It will be more to my present purpose to ask what reply we ourselves might want to make to immoralism as Plato saw it. We need, however, to think a little about what can even be understood as looking at justice *in itself as it is in the soul*. What is the inside and what the outside here?

It is very easy to put this last question in a way that produces nothing but puzzlement. But I suggest that a couple of analogies can help us. Suppose, for instance, that we think first about friendship among humans as this might appear to some not very intelligent visiting Martians who, without being able to talk to us or read our literature or philosophy, have been studying the phenomenon of friendship here on earth. They report that certain humans are linked with certain others in performing what seem to be services, unpaid except by reciprocity. The tacit arrangement seems to be that if humans A and B are friends each is able to call on the other when in difficulties, and there may be exchanges of gifts. Both the services and the gift-giving can be a considerable nuisance to the giver. He or she apparently performs them because everyone needs friends, except perhaps for a very few who are especially rich and powerful. The ordinary needy human would prefer to be like these few, but in fear of friendlessness settles for the next best thing, which is to be a friend and so to be able to call on friends. The institution serves him, and so he praises it.

These Martians would see friendship very much as Plato's immoralists see justice. In itself acting as a friend is, the Martians suppose, disagreeable, like gymnastic exercise or medical treatment.

For the run of humans it is, however, worthwhile for its rewards. Were it possible to get these rewards by gaining the reputation of being a friend without really accepting its duties, that is what any human would seek. The point of my analogy lies, of course, in the fact that these Martians would be *failing to understand* what friendship actually is in human life. And if, rather labouring the point, we described the way in which they have got things wrong, we should find that without any philosophical intention we had described what friendship *is* in the human mind and heart. What friendship requires a friend to do for a friend may indeed be onerous, involving even life itself. But what is done in friendship is done gladly, *con amore*: perhaps with regret but without resentment about the way the chips have fallen. We ourselves know perfectly well that it is not true that the best life would consist in successfully pretending to friendship: having friends to serve one but without being a real friend oneself. A Thrasymachean view of friendship would instantly be recognized as wrong.

Nor is this an isolated case. A similar analogy could be suggested if the subject were not friendship but rather the relation between parents and children. Here too, unintelligent Martians might think that parents saw looking after children as worthwhile only because children help with the harvest and support parents in old age. And with this example one can see, again, the existence of the concept of *one's own good* that was *on the scene* in the discussion of our Letter-Writers in the previous chapter.[4] A loving parent would often be puzzled if told 'You should just consider your own good' if the good of the children were at stake. Naturally, there can be consideration of advantages on one side or the other, having to do, for instance, with an interesting job for a parent in one country and better schooling for the children elsewhere. But there is a way in which a loving parent does not really separate *his or her good* from the good of the children. And I think it is wrong to suppose that this is only because one will affect the other. Joseph Conrad's story of the sea captain, who happily if ruefully sold his boat (which was day-to-day his whole life) for the sake of sending money to his far-away grown-

[4] See pp. 94–6.

up daughter, may be thought rather sentimental by the critics, but nevertheless rings true.[5] If he cared more deeply about his daughter than about his own future there is a sense in which he could not in his mind oppose his good to hers.

It may of course be questioned whether such analogies can really help us to understand what justice is 'in the soul'. After all, we can hardly think that people pay debts, keep promises, or refrain from taking the goods of others *out of love*! Of course not. Hume, who so much stressed the part played by sympathy in the moral life, had to admit the difficulty of cases like that of paying a debt to a profligate creditor. Nevertheless, it is one of the advantages of the recent interest in virtue theories of ethics that moral philosophers are thinking about virtues rather than bare acts. For Aristotle was surely right to distinguish doing *what* the just man does from doing it *as* the just man does it.[6] Aristotle's stress was mainly on the stability of the principle of true justice; but we might also think of it in terms of the underlying thoughts, feelings, and attitudes of one who recognizes the claim of any human being to a certain kind of respect. Here it is perhaps enough to point out that it makes sense to speak of those who are lovers of justice—as of those who love truth.

The plot thickens, however, if we leap across the centuries to confront the greatest of those who have been called immoralists; that is, to confront Nietzsche. Few contemporary moral philosophers, at least in the analytic tradition, have really joined battle with Nietzsche about morality. By and large we have just gone on taking moral judgements for granted as if nothing had happened. We, the philosopher watchdogs, have mostly failed to bark; which, given Nietzsche's genius and his great and continuing influence, is surely rather odd. For while J. P. Stern surely exaggerates the extent to which Hitler embodied Nietzsche's values,[7] and Nietzsche sometimes spoke out against anti-Semitism, nevertheless the Nazis were able to

---

[5] Conrad, *The End of the Tether*.

[6] Aristotle, *Nicomachean Ethics*, Book II, chapter 4, 1105a26–b9.

[7] Writing of Nietzsche's belief in the unconditioned value of self-realization and self-becoming, he says, 'No man came closer to the full realization of self-created values than A. Hitler': Stern, *Friedrich Nietzsche*, 86.

call on him in defence of their genocidal policies. That alone should wake us up.

I want to challenge Nietzsche. But that is easier said than done, if only because it is hard even to locate the field of battle. Nietzsche called himself an immoralist and said that he was attacking morality itself, but he is not consistent in this and many interpreters have denied that he was really an immoralist. The word does not matter, but it is impossible, I believe, to confront him without separating out at least three distinct theses that might come under this description.

There is, first of all, Nietzsche's insistence that free will is simply an illusion. It has recently been strongly argued that these views on moral responsibility are central to Nietzsche's immoralism because they explain the reach of his attack on morality, beyond 'the morality of pity' to 'morality itself'.[8] I think that this is right, but nevertheless want to put his attack on free will aside. For here Nietzsche's attack was on the idea of a pure substance standing outside nature but nevertheless intervening to cause actions in the world. Perhaps he had in mind something like Kant's Noumenal Self; he was certainly wholly hostile to Kant and Schopenhauer even in their idea of a more real world behind the world of appearances. The denial of free will was indeed a pillar of Nietzsche's attack at least on a certain kind of morality, because he saw such a metaphysic of the self as necessary to the idea of moral responsibility and the morality of desert. To sweep them away would be to destroy the kind of judging, particularly the blaming, that seemed to him to be of the essence of morality and to show a detestable love of retribution. Nietzsche loathed the idea of punishment, saying (surely rightly) that we should mistrust anyone in whom an instinct to punish was strong.[9]

Why, then, do I want to leave his denial of free will aside? Because really to threaten morality itself Nietzsche would have had to show not only that free will as he understood it was an illusion,

---

[8] See Clark, 'Nietzsche's Immoralism and the Concept of Morality', in R. Schacht (ed.), *Nietzsche, Genealogy, Morality*, 15–34.

[9] He also thought that many criminals were simply strong men destroyed by society's hatred: 'Skirmishes of an Untimely Man', in *Twilight of the Idols*, 45.

but also that no *other* distinction between voluntary and involuntary action (Aristotle's, for instance) would do instead. He seems to be wrong about this. And perhaps he is also wrong in thinking that moral evaluation of voluntary action and character requires the kind of attribution of responsibility that he thinks of as the moral way of judging, and speaks of as essentially unfair. Bernard Williams, discussing Nietzsche, says:

> Reminded both that different pictures of action have been held in other cultures, and that the notion of action itself is less than transparent, we can be helped to see that the integrity of action, the agent's genuine presence in it, can be preserved without this picture of the will.[10]

If this is right, it is not Nietzsche's metaphysic of the soul that is most important to one who believes, as I do, that we should take the threat of his immoralism seriously, and wants to ask how it might be met.

For this reason I shall now turn to a different strand in Nietzsche's immoralism, to the attack on specifically Christian morality, which was especially prominent in his earlier writings—for instance, in *Human, All Too Human*. Here, when Nietzsche called himself an immoralist or attacked morality, his target was primarily what he called 'pity morality'. That is to say, it was the Christian teaching that he identified especially with 'herd morality', the morality of 'the weak and inferior' who, while secretly cruel and above all resentful, performed acts of 'kindness' with which they would demean the recipient and bolster up their own self-esteem.[11]

All this has to be taken seriously because Nietzsche can claim, almost equally with Freud, who admired him greatly, to be the founder of the theory of depth psychology. In this vein he makes observations impossible to dismiss. He recognized only Dostoevsky as his superior, claiming himself to be an innovating genius in the field. And indeed Nietzsche's psychological insights have rightly

---

[10] Williams, 'Nietzsche's Minimalist Moral Psychology', in R. Schacht (ed.), *Nietzsche, Genealogy, Morality*, 246.

[11] For a fuller description of Nietzsche's doctrines see Foot, 'Nietzsche: The Revaluation of Values', in R. Solomon (ed.), *Nietzsche*, 156–68, and 'Nietzsche's Immoralism', in R. Schacht (ed.), *Nietzsche, Genealogy, Morality*, 3–14.

won him many admirers. He saw the frequent insincerity of profes-
sions of altruism, and the vanity and malice that lurks behind many
of our kindly everyday actions. But of course he goes much further
than this. He says that we do kindnesses to others so as to make
them think well of us, then buy back this good opinion to soothe
our self-hatred. We relieve our dullness with tales of others' misfortune. We torment others by displaying our virtues. Meanwhile,
above all, we ourselves are resentful of our need to accept morality's
control.

At this point Nietzsche's immoralism is like that of Thrasymachus, and that of Plato's other immoralist Callicles in the *Gorgias*,
because supposedly good and admirable characters are depicted as
weak and therefore as objects of scorn. And Nietzsche's attack, if
sustainable, would be more deadly than the others, just because he
is speaking in sophisticated ways of what acts of justice and charity
are in the soul. He is thus trespassing on the very ground of Plato's
own defence against Thrasymachus; he is representing a moral man
as a wretched, fearful creature, tormented by a biting conscience
and unable to seek his own good. The morality of pity, which is not
even helpful to others, is above all harmful to the moral man himself. Like Callicles, Nietzsche sees human beings as tamed by morality and, like tamed animals, as thereby reduced.[12] He represents
human good in terms of individuality, spontaneity, daring, and a
kind of creativity that rejects the idea of a rule of life that would be
valid for others as well. Members of 'the herd' are, by contrast, con-
forming, fawning, propitiating, 'dog-like' creatures. They settle for a
banal kind of happiness; they 'have little pleasures for the day and
little pleasures for the night; and they take good care of their
health'.[13]

What are we to make of these charges against Christian morality?
Anyone who is sympathetic to the representation of human goodness as 'natural goodness', as that has been described in the present

---

[12] Apparently Nietzsche was influenced by Plato's portrait of Callicles. But he
would not at all have agreed with Callicles that the man who is to act rightly 'should
let his appetites grow as large as possible . . . and to fill them with whatever he has
appetite for at any time'. Plato, *Gorgias*, 491E5–492A3.

[13] Nietzsche, *Thus Spake Zarathustra*, Zarathustra's Prologue, section 5.

book, must take them very seriously indeed. For what Nietzsche is denying of the supposed virtue of charity is exactly *the connection with human good that was earlier said to give a character trait that status.* Taking pity (*Mitleid*) to be at the core of Christianity, he insisted that it was a kind of sickness, harmful to pitied and pitier alike. He claimed that this morality was 'slave morality' and said that it grew out of the resentment felt by the weak on account of their inferiority. Nietzsche described resentment (*Ressentiment*) as 'aggrieved conceit, repressed envy'.[14] As Robert Solomon has put it, 'frustration lies at the heart of *Ressentiment*, its description often embodies such metaphors . . . as "simmering," "seething," and "fuming".'[15]

This is strong stuff. For it goes without saying that one consumed by *Ressentiment* lives a wretched life—that Christian morality seen like this has a systematic connection not with happiness but rather with frustration, and of course with deprivation of the kind of creativity, freedom, and lightness of spirit that Nietzsche rightly sees as a great part of human good. But does one really have to see a morality that stresses the humanness of sympathy—Hume's, for instance—as mistaken? Are those whose compassion for the unfortunate may even go so far as to rule their lives really to be seen as thereby expressing a twisted sense of inferiority? Is charity really mostly a sham? Sometimes, of course, it may be a sham, and Nietzsche, with his devilish eye for hidden malice and self-aggrandizement and for acts of kindness motivated by the wish to still self-doubt, arouses a wry sense of familiarity in most of us. But this is not to say that there is not a great deal of genuine charity—of the genuine virtue—in people who do not at all fit the picture Nietzsche draws of those master types who hold themselves at a distance from the Christian 'herd'. Thinking of the ordinary unpretentious men and women who seem to find special happiness in working for the relief of suffering, one must surely find Nietzsche's dismissive views on compassion rather silly.

To say this is not, however, to reject the depth psychology that is

[14] Ibid. Part II, 'On the Spirit of the Tarantulas'.
[15] Robert Solomon, 'One Hundred Years of *Ressentiment*', in R. Schacht (ed.), *Nietzsche, Genealogy, Morality*, 103.

more or less taken for granted nowadays. Perhaps most of us can now come to terms with the thought that our motives are seldom without any trace of vanity or self-regard. Perhaps today we can recognize how much of malice, vanity, and even aggression is often present in what we do, without drawing an immoralist conclusion. A story is told of an old priest, who, asked if he had learned anything about human beings in his many years of hearing confessions, first said 'No', but then, 'Yes. There are no grown-ups.' Is it not possible to think that he spoke truly, acknowledging the greedy, jealous, small child that is ever with us, and yet insist that genuine kindness exists? If so, by the criteria of natural normativity charity is a prime candidate as a virtue, because love and other forms of kindness are needed by every one of us when misfortune strikes, and may be a sign of strength rather than weakness in those who are sorry for us. We may reasonably think, moreover, that charity makes for happiness in the one who has it, as hardness does not.

We are now, of course, in an area in which philosophy can claim no special voice: facts about human life are in question and so no philosopher has a special right to speak. But we can use Nietzsche's attack on 'the morality of pity' to unravel a tangle that may otherwise ensnare us when we try to confront him. For we often find in his writings a claim that he is engaged on 'the revaluation of values', and this is a confusing idea. What could it mean to revalue values? By what values are the values to be revalued? And can these values be revalued in their turn?

We shall not, I think, get anywhere by asking questions in which such abstractions appear out of context.[16] But if we look at what was going on in Nietzsche's attack on Christian morality as he conceived it, the puzzle disappears. He was saying that something thought good was not really good: 'Pity is thought good but is not really good.' Here we have the 'X is good' form that does not in general give a determinate thought.[17] But clearly what is in question is whether pity is a disposition that *should* be cultivated or rather

---

[16] Wittgenstein, *Philosophical Investigations*, section 116: 'What *we* do is to bring words back from their metaphysical to their everyday use.'

[17] Compare my objections to G. E. Moore in the Introduction to this book.

avoided in human life; that is, whether someone is to be seen as a good person in so far as he or she feels compassion for others, or rather the reverse as Nietzsche suggests. He is focusing on an evaluative assessment of attitudes and feelings that he finds in Christian morality. He is denying the proposition 'To pity others is to have a good disposition towards them', and so is challenging a judgement about what I have called natural goodness and defect in the human species.

How are we to understand such a challenge? To set it in the right conceptual framework one might usefully compare his challenge with an evaluation that has to do with a characteristic found in a species of animal, for instance, the dancing operation in honey bees. The dancing of a homecoming bee leads other bees to a source of nectar and so plays a beneficial role in the life of the hive. But at one time this supposition was queried. So suppose it were not true after all that other bees found nectar by reacting to the movements of an individual returning to the hive; in that case, unless the dance played a part in the life of the dancer itself, unless it was something that a homecomer needed to do for its own good, there would be no merit in a bee's dancing and no 'natural defect' in an individual bee just because it did not dance.

This outlines a procedure in which an evaluation might be revalued, and the procedure is in principle no different when an evaluation of a characteristic or an operation of human beings is in question. It might have been thought, for example, that it was good for human beings to be as fat as possible, before it was realized that corpulence went with ill-health. And in our own lifetime extant moral beliefs about various sexual practices have come to many of us to seem mistaken; we have re-evaluated old beliefs about the baneful influence of, for instance, masturbation or homosexuality, and so revised former evaluations. If we take this as an example of revaluing values, we can look at Nietzsche's attack on Christian values more or less on his own terms. He asked whether pity was good for the one pitying or the one pitied, and this was the right question to ask. To be sure, his treatment of the topic was all mixed up with gratuitous contempt for the kind of human beings he saw as inferiors and some pretty strange ideas about the resentment and hidden malice of those who accept conventional moral restraints. I have suggested that he got his facts wrong; but if his facts had been right, his revaluation of pity would have been right as well. To some extent I suppose that Nietzsche was indeed right if we are thinking, strictly speaking, of what we call 'pity'. For we may think that no one really likes being pitied. It is rather what we call compassion that is respectful and good.[18]

So much, then, for Nietzsche's attack on what he had labelled 'pity morality'. The theme continued throughout his writings; but increasingly, as time went on, he moved to a different and more sinister point of view, in that he went so far as to deny 'intrinsic badness' in the doing of any kind of act. In *The Genealogy of Morals*, published in 1887, he wrote:

> To talk of intrinsic right and wrong is absolutely nonsensical: intrinsically, an injury, an oppression, an exploitation, an annihilation can be nothing wrong, in as much as life is *essentially* . . . something which functions by injuring, oppressing, exploiting, and annihilating, and is absolutely incomprehensible without such a character.[19]

The reason given here as to why no action can be intrinsically wrong is not one that we can take very seriously, because it depends on an illicit identification of features of the plant and animal worlds with *human acts* of injury or oppression. We must look for a more interesting and original argument than this, and indeed that is to be found in a part of Nietzsche's theory of psychology that is more radical and more threatening than anything I have touched on so far. His most deeply rooted thought about the goodness and badness of human actions was based on something we might label 'psychological individualism', or perhaps 'personalism'. He thought profoundly mistaken a taxonomy that classified actions as the doing of this or that, insisting that the true nature of an action depended rather on *the nature of the individual who did it*. (I think he must have seen a classification under descriptions such as 'murder' or 'oppression'

---

[18] For a discussion of the meaning of *Mitleid* in Nietzsche, see Kaufmann, *Nietzsche*, 363–71. Also Salaquarda, 'Nietzsche and the Judaeo-Christian Tradition', in *The Cambridge Companion to Nietzsche*, 90–118.

[19] Nietzsche, *The Genealogy of Morals*, Second Essay, section 11

rather as Linnaeus must have seen previous taxonomies of plants, or as a scientist conversant with the classification of metals by their molecular structure might see the taxonomies of alchemy.)

A denial of the intrinsic badness of kinds of actions may, of course, look like nothing more than the common (though I myself believe mistaken) belief that there are no *kinds* of actions, however horrific, that could not in extreme circumstances be justified by a pressing end.[20] But it is more than this. Nietzsche was speaking about injury and oppression; using descriptions tending to imply that such arguably extenuating circumstances were not on the scene. In any case his own thought was different. It was that right and wrong in action could not be determined by *what* was done *except in so far as that stood in a certain relation to the particular nature of the person who performed it*. Thus, while he was ready to castigate certain types of individuals as cruel monsters or licentious beasts (having no time for either), he spoke indulgently of the nobles of earlier times, whom he saw as 'pranksome' (*spöttisch*) in performing acts of plunder, murder, and rape.[21]

The fact that he said such things might incline us to say that Nietzsche was undoubtedly an immoralist. But perhaps the sense of that word as applied to Nietzsche is not as clear as it once seemed to be. For he was, after all, ready to endorse what we may be inclined to see as moral judgements on *types* of human beings, as he notably did in speaking scornfully of the merely licentious, as contrasted with those who undertook the noble task of forming in themselves a body of strong but controlled and disciplined passions. Indeed we might give a list of Nietzschean virtues, putting courage and integrity at the head of that list and, on the other side, Nietzschean vices such as the malice and inauthenticity that he attributed to 'members of the herd'. But even in this part of his work he attacked deeply rooted moral views, because he gave the 'affects' of cruelty and lust (the dark passions) an essential place in human life. He seemed to think them especially necessary for the transformation to a higher form of human being that he believed possible—if only

---

[20] See pp. 77–80, 114–15.
[21] Nietzsche, *The Genealogy of Morals*, First Essay, section 11.

people would listen to him. The image of the tree that had to grow
with its roots in the mud worked powerfully in Nietzsche's mind,
and it must surely have been this part of his philosophy that he was
thinking of when he recognized the hatred that his writings would
arouse, and the dangerousness of the seas of thought on which he
had embarked.[22]

How, one may wonder, did Nietzsche come to this strange position, embraced with such passionate intellectual integrity and a sur-
passing courage that prevented him from shrinking from even the
most dangerous of thoughts? His crucial idea was, I think, about
what constituted a good life for a human being, that is, his idea of
human good. The terms in which he was ready to describe such a
thing were 'creativity', 'self-confidence', 'lightness of spirit', 'daring',
and so forth. But beyond these very general descriptions he thought
that nothing could be said. He spoke with special scorn of the belief
that there could be a good that was not just my good or your good
but 'good and evil the same for all'.[23] He would, perhaps, have
agreed with the basic schema described in earlier chapters of the
present book in so far as he would have thought that a genuine
virtue would have to be such as to fit an individual for his own good.
But where this good lay was, in any specific terms, something that
an individual had to determine for himself, creating his own values
rather than paying heed to anyone else.

Delving further into the origins of this moral taxonomy, we find
that it depended on psychological theories that go far beyond the
observations involved in Nietzsche's attack on 'pity morality' as
described earlier in this chapter. In his theoretical psychology, of
which he was very proud, he asserted the existence of a constella-
tion of drives (*Triebe*) that he thought must underlie the relatively
superficial elements that psychologists so far had had in their sights.
But the truth is that as far as these drives were concerned he had
nothing more to offer than the *concept* of a depth psychology and a
promissory note filled out only with the highly dubious suggestion
that they could all be reduced to a will to power. Freud was by com-

[22] See, for instance, Nietzsche, *The Genealogy of Morals*, Preface, section 6.
[23] Nietzsche, *Thus Spake Zarathustra*, Part III, 'Of the Spirit of Gravity'.

parison an empirical scientist, ready after all to give up his overarching 'pleasure principle' when it conflicted with observed facts. Nietzsche, however, fell into the philosophers' trap of inventing a generalizing theory largely unsupported by observation. It is common to think of him as a wonderful psychologist, but at this point I think that he was not.

There was, I am arguing, no sound basis in psychology for the Nietzschean denial that descriptions of what was done, such as 'injury', 'oppression', or 'annihilation', mark out examples of acts contrary to the virtue of justice—unjust actions—that in themselves are morally wrong. This denial seems to me to be a totally mistaken and moreover poisonous doctrine. It is of course contrary to the principles of natural normativity as expounded in the present book, because there is nothing human beings need more than protection from those who would harm and oppress them. To be sure, it matters a great deal, especially in personal relationships, *how* someone is rather than simply what he or she does. Underlying attitudes and desires have already been recognized as an essential *part* of a virtue.[24] But given the horrors of the past century I think that today it would be especially strange not to see the 'what' of actions as even more important. We have seen such terrible things done in Soviet Russia and Nazi Germany, in Chile, Cambodia, Rwanda, that we cannot but have a sense of the awfulness of *this very fact*. It is no doubt of practical import to us to know what kind of a man can give the orders issued by Hitler, Stalin, Pol Pot, or Pinochet, and the personal evil of the legion of torturers now at their loathsome business in so many countries of the world—if only to know how we ourselves might come to act like that. But we do not need to know anything of that kind before branding the things that were and are still being done as utterly wicked. At this point Nietzsche's insistence on individualistic evaluation seems simply absurd, as if we should need to probe deep into the psychology of a Mengele or an Eichmann before we could evaluate their actions. Thomas Mann was surely right when he said, already in 1947,

[24] See p. 48.

How bound in time, how theoretical too, how inexperienced does Nietzsche's romanticizing about wickedness appear . . . today! We have learned to know it in all its miserableness.[25]

Many have, of course, found Nietzsche's individualism inspiring. It seems to preach, as he himself liked to put it, on the side of life, and needless to say there is some good in this. But those who take his attack on morality simply as a rather edifying call to authenticity and self-fulfilment are deluding themselves; the proof of this lying precisely in what he said about there being no right or wrong in actions considered in themselves. About whom, we may ask, was Nietzsche talking here? He was talking about human beings, not Martians or angels, and, as he used the present tense, about human beings as they are, not about Neanderthal man or man as he may be many millions of years hence. Moreover, the evaluations he is making are about human goodness and defect, so that if the main thesis of the present book is correct the schema of natural normativity will be in place.

It follows that we have to take actual human life into account, and so to think about what men and women would be tempted to do in the absence of moral teachings. Human life, unlike the life of animals, is lived according to norms that are known and taken as patterns by those whose norms they are. So we have to teach children what they may and may not do. Nor could these norms be taught simply by telling children that they are to be courageous and 'authentic', however important it is to encourage them to be daring and also to allow them to discover their true desires. The norms to be followed must largely be formulated in terms of the prohibition of *actions* such as murder or theft. In human life it is an Aristotelian necessity (something on which our way of life depends) that if, for instance, a stranger should come on us when we are sleeping he will not think it all right to kill us or appropriate the tools that we need for the next day's work. In human life as it is, this kind of action is not made good by authenticity or self-fulfilment in the one who does it. Some generally wrong actions are, it is true, justified by special circumstances, as promise-breaking sometimes is; or justified by

---

[25] Mann, *Nietzsche's Philosophy in the Light of Recent Events*, 35.

a special role, such as that of a magistrate or parent. But in admitting this we are getting nowhere near to Nietzsche's denial of the intrinsic rightness or wrongness of kinds of actions, a denial that seems to me to be a totally false doctrine, tempting those who see themselves as exceptional to think that when *they* murder and torture they are doing nothing wrong.[26]

Of course we must take Nietzsche's attacks on morality seriously. He was engaged, as he insisted, on a revaluation of values. And this is not an incomprehensible enterprise. For, unlike the members of other species, humans, having the power of abstract thought, can *consider* their own ways of going on. We humans have ourselves developed and can criticize our own practices. We can ask whether human life might not be better conducted if Nietzsche's doctrines were taught. But then we must think about *how* human life could be carried on. Nietzsche believed that under his influence a higher type of man could develop on earth, and wrote as if he could imagine this new being: as if he saw the possibility of a new species or life form that could develop from our own. My point is that it is only for a different species that Nietzsche's most radical revaluation of values could be valid. It is not valid for us as we are, or are ever likely to be.

[26] For a description of how this came about in the case of the Nazis, see Jonathan Glover's very interesting book, *Humanity*, 316–64.

Postscript

I have been asked the very pertinent question as to where all this leaves disputes about substantial moral questions. Do I really believe that I have described a method for settling them all? The proper reply is that in a way nothing is settled, but everything is left as it was. The account of vice as a natural defect merely gives a framework within which disputes are said to take place, and tries to get rid of some intruding philosophical theories and abstractions that tend to trip us up. There is nothing in the idea of natural normativity that should disturb the good work that many philosophers have recently done, for instance, on problems in medical ethics having to do, for instance, with distinctions between doing and allowing, or again on the doctrine of double effect.

It may be thought that in one area at least there must be a greater knock-on effect. It may seem that the suggestion of a form of goodness common to all living things must carry implications about the way we should treat animals and even plants. But this is a complete misapprehension. Moral philosophy has to do with the conceptual form of certain judgements about human beings, which cover a large area of human activities. Thoughts about cruelty to animals, or about the wanton destruction of useful or beautifully ingenious living things, belong within the usual distinctions of virtues and vices. Goethe told his secretary Eckermann of a certain Englishman who, owning an aviary, was so struck one day by the beautiful appearance of a dead bird that he straight away had the rest killed and stuffed. Hardly a crime! And yet there was *something wrong* with that man.

BIBLIOGRAPHY

ADAMS, R. 'Motive Utilitarianism.' *Journal of Philosophy* 73 (1978), 467–81.

AQUINAS, ST THOMAS. *Summa Theologica*, trans. Fathers of the English Dominican Province. New York: Benziger Brothers, 1947.

ANSCOMBE, G. E. M. *Collected Philosophical Papers*. Minneapolis: University of Minnesota Press, 1981.

—— *Intention*. Oxford: Blackwell, 1957.

—— 'Modern Moral Philosophy.' *Philosophy* 35 (1958). Reprinted in Anscombe, *Collected Philosophical Papers*, iii. 26–42.

—— 'On Promising and its Justice.' *Critica* 3.7/8 (1969). Reprinted in Anscombe, *Collected Philosophical Papers*, iii. 10–21.

—— 'On the Source of the Authority of the State.' *Ratio* 20.1 (1978): 1–28. Reprinted in Anscombe, *Collected Philosophical Papers*, 130–55.

—— 'Practical Inference.' In R. Hursthouse, G. Lawrence, and W. Quinn (eds.), *Virtues and Reasons* (q.v.), 1–34.

—— 'Rules, Rights, and Promises.' *Midwest Studies in Philosophy* 3 (1978): 318–23. Reprinted in Anscombe, *Collected Philosophical Papers*, iii. 92–103.

—— 'The Two Kinds of Error in Action.' *Journal of Philosophy* 60 (1963). Reprinted in Anscombe, *Collected Philosophical Papers*, iii. 3–9.

ARISTOTLE. *Nicomachean Ethics*, trans. H. Rackham. Loeb Classical Library. Cambridge, Mass.: Harvard University Press, 1926.

AYER, A. J. *Language, Truth and Logic*. London: Gollancz, 1936.

BENTHAM, JEREMY. *An Introduction to the Principles of Morals and Legislation*, ed. W. Harrison. Oxford: Blackwell, 1960.

BLACKBURN, S. 'Wise Feelings, Apt Reading' (review of A. Gibbard, *Wise Choices, Apt Feelings*). *Ethics* 102 (1992): 342–56.

—— *Oxford Dictionary of Philosophy*. Oxford: Oxford University Press, 1994.

CLARK, M. 'Nietzsche's Immoralism and the Concept of Morality.' In R. Schacht (ed.), *Nietzsche, Genealogy, Morality* (q.v.), 15–34.

CONRAD, JOSEPH. *The End of the Tether*. Everyman's Library. London: J. M. Dent, 1967.

DAVIDSON, D. 'How is Weakness of the Will Possible?' Reprinted in Davidson, *Essays on Actions and Events*. Oxford: Clarendon Press, 1980, 21–42.

DAWKINS, R. *The Extended Phenotype*. Oxford: Oxford University Press, 1982.

DOSTOEVSKY, FEDOR. *The Brothers Karamazov*, trans. Edward Garnet. Everyman's Library. London: J. M. Dent, 1927.

—— *Notes from the Underground*, in *Three Short Novels of Dostoevsky*, trans. Constance Garnet. New York: Doubleday, 1960.

DWORKIN, R. 'Report from Hell.' *New York Review of Books*, 17 July 1986.

ELIOT, GEORGE. *Middlemarch*. World's Classics. Oxford: Oxford University Press, 1947.

FOOT, P. 'Does Moral Subjectivism Rest on a Mistake?' *Oxford Journal of Legal Studies* 15.1 (1995): 1–14. Reprinted in Roger Teichmann (ed.), *Logic, Cause and Action* (Royal Institute of Philosophy Supplement 46), 107–23. Cambridge: Cambridge University Press, 2000.

—— 'Goodness and Choice.' *Proceedings of the Aristotelian Society* supp. vol. 35 (1961): 45–60. Reprinted in Foot, *Virtues and Vices*, 132–47.

—— 'Moral Beliefs.' *Proceedings of the Aristotelian Society* 59 (1958–9): 83–104. Reprinted in Foot, *Virtues and Vices*, 110–31.

—— 'Moral Dilemmas Revisited.' In W. Sinnott-Armstrong, D. Raffman, and N. Asher (eds.), *Modality, Morality and Belief: Essays in Honour of Ruth Marcus*. Cambridge: Cambridge University Press, 1995.

—— 'Morality as a System of Hypothetical Imperatives.' *Philosophical Review* 81.3 (1972): 305–16. Reprinted in Foot, *Virtues and Vices*, 157–73.

—— 'Nietzsche: The Revaluation of Values.' In R. Solomon (ed.), *Nietzsche: A Collection of Critical Essays* (q.v.), 156–68.

—— 'Nietzsche's Immoralism.' In R. Schacht (ed.), *Nietzsche, Genealogy, Morality* (q.v.), 3–14.

—— 'Reasons for Action and Desire.' *Proceedings of the Aristotelian Society* supp. vol. 46 (1972): 203–10. Reprinted in Foot, *Virtues and Vices*, 148–56.

—— (ed.). *Theories of Ethics*. Oxford: Oxford University Press, 1967.

—— 'Virtues and Vices.' In Foot, *Virtues and Vices*, 1–18.

—— *Virtues and Vices and Other Essays in Moral Philosophy*. Oxford: Blackwell, 1978.

GAUTHIER, D. *Morals by Agreement*. Oxford: Clarendon Press, 1986.

GEACH, P. 'Good and Evil.' *Analysis* 17 (1956): 35–42. Reprinted in Foot (ed.), *Theories of Ethics* (q.v.), 64–73.

—— *The Virtues*. Cambridge: Cambridge University Press, 1977.

GIBBARD, A. *Wise Choices, Apt Feelings*. Cambridge, Mass.: Harvard University Press, 1990.

GIDE, A. *The Immoralist*, trans. D. Bussy. New York: A. A. Knopf, 1930.

GLOVER, J. *Humanity*. London: Random House, 1999.

GOLLWITZER, H., KUHN, K., and SCHNEIDER, R. (eds.). *Dying We Live*, trans. R. Kuhn. London: Harvill Press, 1956.

HARDY, T. *Tess of the D'Urbervilles*. World's Classics. Oxford: Oxford University Press, 1983.

HARE, R. M. *Freedom and Reason*. Oxford: Clarendon Press, 1963.

—— *The Language of Morals*. Oxford: Clarendon Press, 1952.

—— *Moral Thinking*. Oxford: Clarendon Press, 1981.

—— 'Objective Prescriptions.' In A. P. Griffiths (ed.), *Ethics* (Royal Institute of Philosophy Lectures, 1993). Cambridge: Cambridge University Press, 1994. Reprinted in Hare, *Objective Prescriptions and Other Essays*. Oxford: Clarendon Press, 1999, 1–18.

—— 'Off on the Wrong Foot.' *Canadian Journal of Philosophy* supp. vol. 21. Reprinted as 'Philippa Foot on Subjectivism' in Hare, *Objective Prescriptions and Other Essays*. Oxford Clarendon Press, 1999, 87–95.

HEINAMAN, R. (ed.). *Aristotle and Moral Realism*. London: UCL Press, 1995.

HUME, DAVID. *An Enquiry Concerning the Principles of Morals*, ed. L. A. Selby-Bigge. Oxford: Clarendon Press, 1936.

—— *A Treatise of Human Nature*, ed. L. A. Selby-Bigge. Oxford: Clarendon Press, 1946.

HURSTHOUSE, R. *On Virtue Ethics*. Oxford: Oxford University Press, 1999.

HURSTHOUSE, R., LAWRENCE, G., and QUINN, W. (eds.). *Virtues and Reasons*. Oxford: Clarendon Press, 1995.

JONES, J. *Dostoevsky*. Oxford: Clarendon Press, 1983.

KANT, IMMANUEL. *Foundations of the Metaphysic of Morals*, trans. T. K. Abbott. London: Longmans, 1946.

KAUFMANN, W. *Nietzsche: Philosopher, Psychologist, Antichrist*. New York: Vintage Press, Random House, 1968.

KORSGAARD, C. 'Scepticism about Practical Reason.' *Journal of Philosophy* 83.1 (1986): 5–25.

KROPOTKIN, P. *Memoirs of a Revolutionist*. New York: Dover, 1971.

LAWRENCE, G. 'The Rationality of Morality.' In Hursthouse, Lawrence, and Quinn (eds.), *Virtues and Reasons* (q.v.), 89–147.

—— 'Reflection, Practice and Scepticism.' *Pacific Philosophical Quarterly* 74 (1993): 289–361.

LOCKE, JOHN. *An Essay concerning Human Understanding*, ed. P. H. Nidditch. Oxford: Clarendon Press, 1975.

MACKIE, J. *Ethics: Inventing Right and Wrong*. Harmondsworth: Penguin, 1977.

McDOWELL, J. 'Are Moral Requirements Hypothetical Imperatives?' *Proceedings of the Aristotelian Society* supp. vol. 52 (1978): 13–29.

—— 'Eudaimonism and Realism in Aristotle's Ethics.' In R. Heinaman (ed.), *Aristotle and Moral Realism* (q.v.), 201–18.

—— 'The Role of *Eudaimonia* in Aristotle's Ethics.' In A. Rorty (ed.), *Essays on Aristotle's Ethics* (q.v.), 359–76.

MACAULAY, THOMAS BABINGTON. *The History of England*. London: J. M. Dent, 1906.

MALCOLM, N. *Ludwig Wittgenstein: A Memoir*. Oxford: Oxford University Press, 1984.

MANN, T. *Nietzsche's Philosophy in the Light of Recent Events*. Washington, D.C.: Library of Congress, 1947.

MILL, JOHN STUART. *On Liberty*. Everyman's Library. London: J. M. Dent, 1920.

MILLIKAN, R. *Language, Thought, and Other Biological Categories*. Cambridge, Mass.: MIT Press, 1984.

MOORE, G. E. *Principia Ethica*. Cambridge: Cambridge University Press, 1903.

NAGEL, T. *The Possibility of Altruism*. Oxford: Clarendon Press, 1970.

NIETZSCHE, FRIEDRICH. *The Gay Science*, trans. W. Kaufmann. New York: Vintage Books, 1974.

—— *Human, All Too Human*, trans. M. Faber and S. Lehman. Lincoln: University of Nebraska Press, 1984.

—— *On the Genealogy of Morals*, trans. W. Kaufmann. New York: Vintage Books, 1967.

—— *The Portable Nietzsche*, ed. W. Kaufmann. New York: Viking, 1954.

—— *Thus Spake Zarathustra*, trans. W. Kaufmann. In Nietzsche, *The Portable Nietzsche*, 121–439.

—— *Twilight of the Idols*, trans. W. Kaufmann. In Nietzsche, *The Portable Nietzsche*, 464–563.

NIJINSKY, R. *Nijinsky*. New York: Simon & Schuster, 1972.

PARFIT, D. *Reasons and Persons*, Oxford: Oxford University Press, 1984.

PLATO. *Gorgias*, trans. W. Lamb. Loeb Classical Library. Cambridge, Mass.: Harvard University Press, 1991.

—— *Republic*, trans. P. Shorey. Loeb Classical Library. Cambridge, Mass.: Harvard University Press, 1930.

PRICHARD, H. A. 'Duty and Interest' (inaugural lecture). Oxford: Oxford University Press, 1928. Reprinted in Prichard, *Moral Obligation*. Paperback edition, Oxford: Oxford University Press, 1968, 201–38.

QUINN, W. 'Putting Rationality in its Place.' In Quinn, *Morality and Action*. Cambridge: Cambridge University Press, 1993, 228–55.

—— 'Rationality and the Human Good.' In Quinn, *Morality and Action*. Cambridge: Cambridge University Press, 1993, 210–17.

RORTY, A. (ed.). *Essays on Aristotle's Ethics*. Berkeley: University of California Press, 1980.

ROSEBERY, LORD. *Pitt*. London: Macmillan, 1899.

SALAQUARDA, J. 'Nietzsche and the Judaeo-Christian Tradition.' In Bernd Magnus and Kathleen Higgins (eds.), *The Cambridge Companion to Nietzsche*. Cambridge: Cambridge University Press, 1996.

SCHACHT, R. (ed.). *Nietzsche, Genealogy, Morality*. Berkeley: University of California Press, 1994.

SEN, A. 'Utilitarianism and Welfarism.' *Journal of Philosophy* 76.9 (1979): 463–89.

SMITH, M. 'The Humean Theory of Motivation.' *Mind* n.s. 96 (1987): 36–61.

SOLOMON, R. (ed.). *Nietzsche: A Collection of Critical Essays*. New York: Anchor Press/Doubleday, 1973.

STATMAN, D. (ed.). *Virtue Ethics*. Edinburgh: Edinburgh University Press, 1997.

STEIN, G. 'The Good Anna.' In Stein, *Three Lives*. New York: Penguin, 1990.

STERN, J. *Friedrich Nietzsche*. New York: Penguin, 1979.

STEVENSON, C. L. *Ethics and Language*. New Haven, Conn.: Yale University Press, 1945.

TAUREK, J. 'Should the Numbers Count?' *Philosophy and Public Affairs* 6.4 (1977): 293–316.

THOMPSON, M. 'The Representation of Life.' In R. Hursthouse, G. Lawrence, and W. Quinn (eds.), *Virtues and Reasons*. Oxford: Clarendon Press, 1995.

WATSON, G. 'On the Primacy of Character.' In D. Statman (ed.), *Virtue Ethics* (q.v.), 56–81.

WIGGINS, D. 'Eudaimonism and Realism in Aristotle's Ethics: A Reply to John McDowell.' In R. Heinaman (ed.), *Aristotle and Moral Realism* (q.v.), 219–31.

—— 'A Sensible Subjectivism?' In Wiggins, *Needs, Values, Truth* (Aristotelian Society Series no. 6). Oxford: Blackwell, 1987, 185–214.

—— 'Postscript 4.' In Wiggins, *Needs, Values, Truth* (Aristotelian Society Series no. 6). Oxford: Blackwell, 1987, 351–6.

WILLIAMS, B. *Ethics and the Limits of Philosophy*. London: Fontana/Collins, 1985.

—— 'Nietzsche's Minimalist Moral Psychology.' In R. Schacht (ed.), *Nietzsche, Genealogy, Morality* (q.v.), 237–47.

WITTGENSTEIN, LUDWIG. *Philosophical Investigations*. Oxford: Blackwell, 1953.

—— *Remarks on the Philosophy of Psychology*. Oxford: Blackwell, 1980.

INDEX

CPSIA information can be obtained at www.ICGtesting.com
Printed in the USA
BVOW031358131211

278245BV00005B/13/P